THE GENTLE ART OF LEXICOGRAPHY

THE GENTLE ART OF
LEXICOGRAPHY

as pursued and experienced by an addict

Eric Partridge

I am not so lost in lexicography as to forget that words are the daughters of earth, and that things [*including deeds*] are the sons of heaven.

Samuel Johnson, in the Preface of his *Dictionary*, 1755.

THE MACMILLAN COMPANY
NEW YORK

Printed in Great Britain

© Eric Partridge 1963

Library of Congress Catalog Card No 63-12833

For
Eileen and Anna:
the two most intelligent,
delightful and talented
girls I know.

CONTENTS

PREFACE

✱✱

WHEN MR AL HART of the Macmillan Company, Inc., invited me to launch upon the perilous waters of *belles-lettres* a small barque carrying a cargo of lexicography, I recoiled in alarm, for I could not, at a first rapid inspection, see how the frail craft could possibly survive the Scylla of a formidably specialist subject and the Charybdis of competition with such professionals as Professor J. R. Hulbert (*Dictionaries, British and American*) and Professor Ladislas Országh and Dr R. W. Chapman and several others. Merely to summarize and generalize what they have so pertinently and authoritatively written would be not merely a crass supererogation but an unwarrantable impertinence.

Yet the thought of writing a small book on lexicography – something rather less 'popular', rather more systematic and much more comprehensive, than the essay appearing, 1952, in *From Sanskrit to Brazil* – had occurred to me more than once during the period that has elapsed since *Origins* appeared, late in 1958; only to be dismissed as, on brief consideration, impracticable – for the above-mentioned reasons. Mr Hart, the most insidious and urbane of *agents provocateurs*, said, 'Well, think it over.' I did: and the solution at which I eventually arrived was this.

Instead of attempting a compact *multum in parvo* that would satisfy neither the scholars nor the intelligent public; instead of wrestling with a mass of irrefutable principles and repellent technicalities; instead of wallowing in an academic exercise of illusive impartiality and complacent competence; and instead of flattering myself that I might be helping others: abandoning all such noble aims, I could present lexicography in the light of one man's experience of it – the impact or, rather, series of impacts upon him – and the difficulties he encountered and the means he employed to overcome them; I could even try to convey some idea of the human aspect of this arduous, interminable, subtle and Sisyphean art, by describing, not too pompously, the long road I have travelled and by touching briefly upon a few of the persons I have met by the way. This latter course is very much less haphazard and arbitrary than it may seem: *Solvitur ambulando.*

There remains for me to thank, warmly and gratefully, the following publishers for their prompt permission to outline, as examples of alphabetical order and arrangement, their entries for the word *set* and its derivatives: the Clarendon Press (*The Shorter Oxford English Dictionary*); the G. & C. Merriam Company (*Webster's New International Dictionary*, 2nd edition; the order varies slightly in their recent 3rd edition); Messrs W. & R. Chambers, Ltd (*Chambers's Twentieth Century Dictionary*); and Messrs Routledge & Kegan Paul, Ltd (*A Dictionary of Slang and Unconventional English*). Without those generous permissions, Chapter IV would have been a poor and meatless thing. The Clarendon Press has also very kindly allowed me to quote from Dr

R. W. Chapman's *Lexicography*; Messrs John Murray, Ltd, from Ernest Weekley's larger dictionary; and Messrs Routledge & Kegan Paul, from *Origins*.

ERIC PARTRIDGE

I: HOW IT ALL BEGAN

As ONE might expect, Dr Johnson has permitted himself three or four remarks upon lexicography or the art of writing dictionaries. As one might expect, they tend to be both wry and dry. Like most great – as opposed to merely famous – men, he was modest and humble.

'Dictionaries,' he once said, 'are like watches: the worst is better than none, and the best cannot be expected to go quite true'. He defined *lexicographer* as 'a writer of dictionaries' and characteristically added the words, 'a harmless drudge'. Within his great work, he exemplified *dull* with the sentence, 'To make dictionaries is dull work'. Even a cursory glance at a few pages of *A Dictionary of the English Language* (1755) shows us that he did not find the word dull; that he did not regard himself as a drudge; that it is unlikely he thought of himself as harmless. But lexicographical hacks are drudges: and the result of their work is dull and lifeless: and they themselves are, one supposes, harmless fellows, who would be so much better employed in compiling pedestrian encyclopaedias – as doubtless many of them are. For me, lexicography is not dull, but exciting; otherwise I should not be writing this little book at all. Nor have I ever been a drudge.

Clearly, when I use the word *dictionary*, I primarily mean

13

a word-book, not a reference work that, for reasons of convenience, is arranged in alphabetical order, as in (say) *A Dictionary of Architecture* – as opposed to *A Dictionary of Architectural Terms*. The dividing-line is sometimes hard to draw; but let us not diverge upon that fascinating theme!

Near the end of a not too dull life, Albert Jay Nock proclaimed: 'As sheer casual reading-matter, I still find the English dictionary the most interesting book in the language' (*Memoirs of a Superfluous Man*, 1943): and that's as it should be, for what more fundamental than, what so indispensable as, a dictionary? Nock's proclamation reminds me of the trivial story of that old lady who, on borrowing a dictionary from her municipal library, returned it with the comment, 'A *very* unusual book indeed – but the stories are extremely short, aren't they?' A remark, one feels, rather more applicable to the *Who's Who* of any country whatsoever.

For most of us, a dictionary is hardly a book to read; a good dictionary, however, is a book to browse in. Some dictionaries are so well written that one just goes on and on.

To write such a dictionary has always been my ambition.

I began early in life: and it is the course of my life which, allied to a natural propensity to original sin, has made a lexicographer out of me. Perhaps I should have become one even if I had lived always in one country and always done the same work; but probably the migrations and the changes have pin-pointed the predilection and transformed the advisable into the profitable, and necessity into a virtue – if 'virtue' be the right word. As I look back, I seem to discern

a pattern or, if you prefer, a series of happenings, some push-
ing vulgarly, others slyly nudging, me into a career that,
since 1930, has been predominantly lexicographical. Here I
must enter a caveat. Sometimes I grow a little tired of being
called 'the dictionary man' or 'the word man' or even, as
Edmund Wilson, far too generously and, for once in a well-
integrated life, inaccurately, called me, 'the word king'.

My first book was a slim, privately printed volume of not
at all good verse translations from French poetry, 'way back
in 1914. Ten years later, the next two represented my M.A.
and B.Litt. theses. In 1925-29, I published a collection of
literary essays, some editings of English literature, pseudonymously a volume of short stories. Since 1930, I have – in
addition to lexicographical labours of love – issued eight
collections of essays, one literary, one autobiographical, the
others mainly linguistic; pseudonymously a novel; *Slang
Today and Yesterday: A History and a Study*; small books on
'shaggy dogs' and 'comic alphabets'; *English: A Course for
Human Beings*; *You Have a Point There* (a guide to punctua-
tion and its allies); *What's the Meaning?* (an introduction to
etymology). Admittedly, most of those books deal with one
aspect or another of language; but they are not dictionaries –
and neither, except in alphabetical arrangement, are *Usage
and Abusage* and its offshoot, *The Concise Usage and Abusage*.

Nor is that caveat a mere interpolation; much less is it a
self-indulgent effluence of egocentricity. It bears very closely
on much of what is to follow. Much of what follows would
be inexplicable or, at the least, perplexing without the caveat.
After all, I'm a writer and therefore unlikely to fall over my
own feet as I this simple tale unfold.

Born, 1894, in New Zealand, I passed the first ten-or-so years in a country district (its first white child) situated fifteen miles from a small town. Hilly sheep country it was, with a few cattle and only occasional crops, small, domestic. There I naturally gained a pretty intimate knowledge of country life and rural fauna and flora: not the worst basis on which to build a solid foundation for an urban and sedentary life devoted mainly to learning.

Learning very early became a passion; it has remained a passion. 'How so, among the hayseeds?' Easily enough. My father was not uneducated. Apart from being quite well-read, he had received a grounding in Greek and Latin and French and he was a far from average mathematician. He introduced me to books as soon as I could read and before I could read well; he encouraged me to read; he showed me (aged seven) how to use a dictionary – I forget which, but probably an Annandale recension of an Ogilvie.

Inadvertently and perhaps a year later, he inculcated an invaluable lexicographical principle: the pundits are not necessarily right even when they're utterly self-confident. I can remember, vividly remember, how, one summer day, he came in to lunch still fuming from an argument he had had with a visiting farmer, who, as one flew by, said 'That's a large bumble bee'. My father maintained that he had never heard it called anything but a humble bee and that '*humble* bee' was correct, '*bumble* bee' incorrect. The visitor asked why it should be described as *humble*; he was told, 'Because it's a large, good-natured bee that doesn't sting'; to which he replied that, on the contrary, it was named '*bumble* bee' for two reasons; it bumbled and blundered about the place and made a booming sound – on a small scale. My father stuck to his opinion. I felt suitably impressed, although not quite as he supposed. Later I somewhat guiltily looked up *humble bee* in the dictionary; it wasn't there. So, disloyally, I tried *bumble bee*, and there it was. At least I had enough sense to refrain from telling my formidable father this; and for years, whenever I saw or heard of a *humble-bumble* bee, I vaguely wondered which of the disputants had been wrong. When, aged fourteen, I could at last consult an authoritative dictionary, I learned – to my delight and ribald amusement – that both of them had been right about the term. *Humble bee* is apparently the earlier: the O.E.D. records it for 1450 and derives it from the now long-obsolete *humble*, to hum or buzz, as a bee does. *Bumble bee* is recorded for 1530, but it probably existed from fifty or more years earlier, and it derives from *bumble*, to boom or to buzz. Etymologically, our visitor was almost right; my father, entirely wrong. As a result – well, I've already dotted the *i*'s; you may cross the *t*'s.

Yet, before I was quite fourteen, I received a still more valuable lesson. In October, 1907, we migrated from New Zealand to Australia, my father having wearied of the life of 'retired gentleman'; that life had lasted for three years, much to the surprise of my mother and her family, for he was a very active, somewhat restless, decidedly energetic person.

Well, there was I, with a tolerable vocabulary possessing a ruddy New Zealand complexion; cast upon a world so different as to startle anyone except a mature philosopher – and I was neither mature nor philosophical. Although only twelve hundred miles apart, New Zealand and Australia are 'poles apart' in physical composition and nature; in fauna and flora; in climate; ethnically, in respect of their native peoples; and in the very character of the white populations, with their fundamentally different history of settlement and early growth and with the tremendous influence of environments differing so sharply. Not least of the differences was that in speech; a difference of accent and tempo, of intonation and enunciation. The difference in vocabulary was perhaps even greater: new names to learn for the beasts and the reptiles, the birds and the fishes; for the trees and shrubs and grasses; for the soils and the winds; for customs and occupations and, in short, a new way of life. One of the first things I noticed was that what had, in New Zealand, been called a public school was, in Queensland, a State school or, as I learned very much later, a primary school, not necessarily elementary; to add to the confusion, I had somewhere read that, in Britain, a public school or, rather, a Public School was a very superior sort of secondary school – a glorified grammar school. I realised, perhaps for the first time vividly, that, in these questions of nomenclature, it was no good guessing: one had to *know*.

I bought a little note-book and industriously entered all those strange names and words and phrases which came my way or which I learned by eager inquiry. 'If you wish to know, ask!' Probably I made a damned nuisance of myself; certainly my youth protected me from the rude answers some of my informants must have felt very much tempted to make. Most people respond very kindly to a starry-eyed innocence and an ingenuous enthusiasm. Luckily my father had an equally inquiring mind; luckily he perceived that my motive was less daft than it seemed. That spirit of inquiry has served me well throughout my life. By the time I was sixteen or thereabouts, I possessed a technique rather more subtle, much more indirect: but as it's one that might not work with most, nor even with many, I shall not divulge it: thus I shall spare the naïve investigator a busted nose or an indelicate recommendation. (Until the Second World War, most of us regarded ourselves either as inquirers or, if we were scientists or thesis-writers, as researchers; nowadays, the 'inquirer' has become an 'investigator' or a 'field-worker'. The language of simple, honest inquiry has become pompous and pretentious; and so have many of the inquirers.)

Language, however, has an aspect that, in the main, is insusceptible of inquiry, except from oneself and one's reading and one's constant observation of speech, especially of intelligent and preferably educated speech: the *way* in which words are used, by means of syntax, phrasing, idiom, and so forth, to express need or action, thought or meditation, dream or aspiration. Here, the differences between one country and another, one district and another, one occupation and another, one social class and another, and, in one person, between childhood and youth, youth and maturity, are less readily grasped and analysed and systematized – if, indeed, they can be systematized at all. Linked with these features of language are those of differences of meaning; it is exceedingly difficult to prevent the connotations and implications of words, as opposed to their denotations (themselves difficult enough, heaven knows!), from slipping through the semantic net, no matter how finely and cunningly it is meshed. Australian syntax and semantics, phrasing and idiom, I soon perceived, differed appreciably from those of New Zealand. Thus it was that, early in – and throughout – my teens, I became aware of and, at first, perplexed by one of the most delicate characteristics of language: usage; hence, by comparison, abusage too. From usage, one may pass to the perilous and exciting game of attempting to determine sociological and racial characteristics by a searching examination and comparison of accidence and syntax, words and phrases and idioms. If one does, one has to guard against nationalist prejudice and preoccupation. Several otherwise excellent dictionaries have been vitiated by national prejudice, as for instance Noah Webster's by his intensely anti-British bias or Friedrich Kluge's by an almost pathological phobia against everything non-Germanic in general and against everything Semitic in particular. Not, of course, by Kluge (1856–1926) himself, but by Nazi-minded German philologists during the approximate period 1933–1945. The vast majority of words escaped contamination; but all those which could be made, or bent, to subserve the Teutonic dream of world-domination and the constant Teutonic ambition to glorify everything even remotely German and to claim, as German, words or devices or inventions or ideas, not to forget persons, and such human manifestations as they suspected might help to shore up a gigantic fabric of make-believe: all these rather numerous words fell under their malefic sway. All good Germans – for whom scholarship transcended frontiers – squirmed in spiritual discomfort, and a few of them contrived to get out of the country. (But

I did not interest myself in nationalist philology until during the First World War.)

That war ensured a further somewhat drastic development of my linguistic interests. Early in 1915, I enlisted in the Australian Imperial Force and, in May, departed for further training in Egypt. I began my obscure military career as a private in an infantry battalion, with only one blemish. After the Second Australian Division's 'first Pozières', I was the only 'Anzac' left in my section; in a frail moment, I was persuaded to lead the section, a week later, into 'the second Pozières' (4 August, 1916). Much good it did either the section or myself. Crossing No Man's Land, I 'stopped one'. On returning to the battalion some months later, I kept quiet about my promotion to the dizzy rank of lance-corporal and, although several times urged to take a commission, I successfully resisted the influences endangering my independence. Nor was I being entirely unselfish: I'd have made a very poor officer, for I hate to boss people about.

Nor is that a digression. As a private, I learned much more about Australian speech, about Australian English, than I could possibly have done as an officer. I was meeting all the roughs and the toughs, as well as many decent fellows coming from trades and professions of which I knew nothing – or so little as to be worse than nothing. Although I had earned my living since I was sixteen, I had, as teacher and then as undergraduate, met only a few different types of mankind: now I was meeting all conceivable types, from the wealthy pastoralist to the petty crook; from the cane-cutter to the 'wharfie'; from the rural storekeeper to the urban shopkeeper; from the book-keeper to the bookmaker; from the journalist to the 'sundowner' and the 'swaggie'; from the Civil Servant to the commercial traveller and the 'con man' proper; from the shearer to the sailor; from the railway official to the tram-driver. Not only meeting but living with them, in conditions where men regard modesty and reticence as unwanted luggage. Having a quick ear, a comparative mind, a retentive memory, and no hesitation in asking for full and precise information whenever I was in doubt and could ask without giving offence, I naturally acquired a considerable store of technical and semi-technical standard Australian English, as well as a not inconsiderable stock of slangy and colloquial and other unconventional words and phrases and senses and idioms. At the time, I was not intending to specialize in – better, to concentrate upon – English: I had left Queensland as a Classic ('Theocritus' Cholmeley had been one of my University teachers); so far as I thought about the matter – survival being or, at the least, seeming rather more important, I assumed that if ever I had the luck to return, with faculties unimpaired, to Australia, I should continue to be a Classic – no bad training for anyone so rash as to study language in general, the English language in particular. To some extent or, rather, to the requisite extent I have remained one, partly urged by inclination and partly driven by conscience. How anyone can pretend to be an adequate philologist or, at any rate, a good etymologist, without possessing a 'pretty useful' knowledge of Greek and Latin, has always defeated me. Oh! I admit that my Latin has become rather, and my Greek very, rusty, but for many years they were something more than a smattering and I can still 'find my way around' in them with a reasonable approximation to comfort and security.

On the other hand, I cannot truthfully say that, during the First World War, I learned very much about the speech-habits of the English and the Welsh, the Scots and the Irish. I played inattentively on the vast periphery of knowledge; I came to know something about, but hardly knew, the extensive, bewilderingly variegated, field into some of whose corners I was later to roam and pry.

But the influence of those war years is a subject upon which I could expatiate until I lost every friend and estranged every acquaintance. I hated that war. Yet it benefited me more than I can tell.

Then in 1921 I came to England and went to Oxford. This meant that I was obliged to habituate myself to yet another way of life – almost another civilization – and to augment and, in some respects, change or modify a vocabulary, a usage, a pronunciation; it was pronunciation which took me the longest. I have not acquired, nor have I wished to acquire, that variety of Standard English pronunciation which is known as Southern, or Public School, English. Mine is one of the Modified Standards. My aim has always been to speak a clear and lucid, rather than a dulcet, English and to write a lucid and expressive, rather than an elegant, English; and to be occasionally subtle, never precious.

As when I had left New Zealand for Australia, so now the task of learning new names in fauna and flora, in urban and in rural life – new social and professional and commercial customs – strange usages and idioms – confronted me, in circumstances enforcing or, at best, rendering advisable a still more thorough and much more speedy adjustment. Such an adjustment, largely conscious, and such an adaptation, partly unconscious, had three results worth mentioning in this brief account of a progress in the study of language and in the practice of lexicography: they considerably enlarged a vocabulary that was, perhaps, already more various than that of most of my coevals; they increased a natural predilection towards the study of language, especially of the English language wherever and however spoken; and they sharpened an innate curiosity about the origins and nature of this or that word, that or this phrase or idiom.

Not that I took my B.Litt. in language. I took it in a literary subject intimately connected with language. (As if one could divorce literature and language!) 'The Influence of English Literature upon the French Romantics.' When, early in 1919, I had returned to Australia, I changed from an honours course in Classics to one in French and English. Perhaps my interests had, during the war years, moved slightly away from Greek and Latin and towards English, with a strong secondary affection for French and other modern languages. An intimate study of French, a language that had fascinated me ever since I was introduced to it as a young boy, certainly refined my study of English; linguistically, I've never been quite the same person since; but then, only an insensitive could have been. Through my work for this degree, I met three very fine scholars: A. J. Carlyle, my supervisor, and my two examiners, Gustave Rudler and David Nichol Smith. Indirectly, I came also to know George Gordon and H. C. K. Wyld, who held the senior chairs in

English Literature and English Language respectively. To enumerate the benefits accruing from acquaintance with two, friendship with three, of those five men would take far too long. It would be difficult, if not impossible, to evaluate the total collective benefit, whether in scholarship or in the imponderables.

II: TRIAL RUNS

❀❀❀❀❀❀❀❀❀❀❀❀❀❀❀❀❀❀❀❀❀❀❀❀❀❀❀❀❀❀❀❀❀❀❀❀

DURING MY rather more than two years at Oxford, I was working not only on the B.Litt. thesis but also on one for my M.A.; 'Eighteenth Century English Romantic Poetry' – a history and, although less, a study, published in 1924. One of the appendices lists the neologisms committed by the English romantic poets, a task that kept me busy much longer than I had expected; nor was it rendered any easier by the fact that *The Oxford English Dictionary* still had some way to go. I certainly didn't think of this checking and counter-checking as lexicography; nor, in fact, was it. It did, however, verge on lexicography. It both showed me how arduous the lexicographer's labours and allowed me a few momentary glimpses of that quiet pleasure, and those rare, incidental excitements, which do something to irradiate the inspissated gloom and to mitigate the tedium. But that is to give an entirely false impression: seldom do I feel tedium, never do I experience gloom, while I'm engaged upon lexicography. Admittedly it entails very much harder work than that of straightforward writing, such (for instance) as this, and immeasurably harder than that of writing fiction. Nor will it profit the carpers to exclaim, 'But what the – do you know about fiction-writing?' It so happens that I have published a novel and a collection of short stories. (The latter, passable; the former, poor stuff. Fiction, clearly, is not my line of country. For one thing, I write it much too easily.)

Probably not more than half a dozen philologists and probably not so many as one lexicographer have looked at, much less used, that appendix. I don't blame them, for I myself have never consulted it. Yet it does represent a definite stage in a slow advance towards clear-cut, no-nonsense, first-hand lexicography. Lacking the advantage of an apprenticeship in the memorable scriptorium of *The O.E.D.*, I've had to learn an immensely difficult art 'the hard way': hacking out a path, dealing as best I could with each new problem as it arose, extending my activities as and when it became either advisable or unavoidable, and often excavating where little or nothing had been done, and if something had been done at all, done haphazardly and, for the most part, very badly.

Genuine, although elementary, lexicography was involved in a book suggested by John Brophy, who had already published an excellent war novel (*The Bitter End*) and who was to write an even better one, concerned, this time, with the Second World War (*Immortal Sergeant*) and whose name had already figured over the imprint of the small firm I founded in 1927 and was to direct until the end of 1931: The Scholartis Press. 'Why don't you and I bring out a book on the subject of Songs and Slang of the British Soldier?' So we did; and with that title. It appeared in 1930 and demanded, flatteringly soon, a second edition, with a third in 1931: John Brophy attended to the songs and most of the English slang; I helped with the songs and contributed the Australian matter. John's was the main share in the new matter of the second edition; mine in the new matter for the third. John also contributed three distinguished essays.

The slang was arranged in dictionary form. In order to avoid the expense of re-setting the book, the new songs and slang terms of the second and third editions were tacked on, as Supplements, to the original version; but the original was itself twice revised and enlarged. The third edition doubled the length of the first. In any edition, *Songs and Slang* is rather hard to find, and it sells at a small premium. I can fairly say that this is a most readable and entertaining book. Its literary merit is due solely to John Brophy; much of its solid merit is also his. The utmost I can claim is a respectable share in the lexicography – especially in the third edition, where the responsibility for the glossary is almost entirely mine. I also had, after the first edition, something to do with the sections devoted to catch-phrases and sayings.

Economy was not the sole reason for the tiered structure of the second and third editions. We, or perhaps only I, wished to show the growth of such a book. We naturally received scores of letters, some indignant and some sympathetic, several abusive, but most of them helpful and precise. To me fell the task of collating the two successive masses of new slang material; John handled the new songs and the sayings. One of the contributors of slang was that soldier who became Field-Marshal Lord Wavell: and thus began a desultory correspondence that lasted almost up to his death. His contributions were always exact, scholarly, informative, as one might expect from one whose knowledge of military lore equalled that of the military historians. And how obliging and agreeable he unfailingly was! On several occasions we arranged to meet in London. Always something – notably the Second World War – arose to prevent him from keeping the appointment. Another contributor, I seem to remember, was J. B. Priestley, although on a much smaller scale. Him, likewise, I have never met, although we belong to the same London club.

Definitely I remember that, among the reviewers of the first edition, one man stood out, for the authoritative nature of what he wrote: and that was Ernest Weekley. On the whole, he liked our book. He remarked that it had a weakness: there were too few etymologies, and several of those few were incorrect. We replied, in print, that we had not intended to include etymologies at all, a rule we had occasionally broken where the origin appeared to be a matter of some general interest to members of our mainly 'old soldier' public, but that, thus admonished, we intended to include a larger proportion of etymologies in 'later editions (if any)'. This we did, in a very modest way.

As a result of that public reply to someone whose work was well-known to us, someone we admired, Professor Weekley wrote to me, recalled that he had once sat on a University selection committee before which I appeared and humorously reminded me that I had declined the position they offered, and ended by inviting me to take tea with him. During the decade 1930–1939, I dined a few times at his London home. I never saw him after 1939. We corresponded, at increasingly longer intervals, right up to a few months before his death.

Like Wavell, he was a shy and modest, yet friendly and helpful, person. We became very good friends. In meagre return for all his kindnesses and his heartening encouragement, I was able to arrange for the publication (1952) of a revised and enlarged edition of his *Concise Etymological Dictionary of Modern English*. His gratitude for that small service embarrassed me acutely, for I owed him so much. True; I owe nothing to his lexicography, whether in aim or in method. For one thing, I like to go much farther back than he allowed himself to go. But I owe much to his essays on particular words and on certain groups of words. I read everything that, in this kind of work, he ever wrote: *The Romance of Words* and *The Romance of Names*; *Words Ancient and Modern* and *More Words*...; *Adjectives and Other Words; Surnames* and *Jack and Jill*. The method and the manner of those books served as a model for the similar books I have written. I have, on the one hand, modified that model; on the other, enlarged it; yet the original is still recognizable in the copy. I have written fewer essays on particular words, and more essays on aspects of language, than he did. He wrote only rarely upon slang, never upon the language of the underworld; I have dealt with them fairly often. The debt, however, is there for all to see, and I have not sought to belittle, much less to hide, that debt. My earliest collection of essays and papers on words and language was *Words, Words, Words!*, published in 1933 and selected from articles and essays that had appeared in weeklies, monthlies, quarterlies, during the preceding two years. The latest, so far, is *A Charm of Words* (1960). Here I have moved perhaps furthest from what might be termed 'the Weekley canon of popular-essay writing upon linguistic matters'; probably in *Adventuring among Words* (1961) only, have I moved farther.

Another debt I owe to Ernest Weekley is this. His very human approach to language has confirmed me in an innate tendency to remember that language, as commonly apprehended, is a human invention, designed to meet a human need, a fact so excruciatingly obvious that you'd think that no one could forget it – yet some philologists do forget it; a human privilege and a human right; the most effectual human means of communication and the richest, most subtle human means of expression. Language cannot be thrust into a vacuum and examined as though it were something existing apart from the people who devised it and the people who use it. To ignore the human origin, the human dependence, the human nexus, is fatal; to underestimate the people-speech interdependence is dangerous, in that such an underestimation will vitiate everything one writes on the subject of general language and particular aspects or phrases or words. One does not need to be a psychiatrist; one does need to be a profoundly sympathetic psychologist. In less pompous language, one needs to understand human beings, especially the way their minds work, their impulses, their longings and their ambitions. It also helps considerably to have a keen sense of humour.

III: GETTING TO GRIPS

❋❋❋❋❋❋❋❋❋❋❋❋❋❋❋❋❋❋❋❋❋❋❋❋❋❋❋❋❋❋❋❋❋❋

THROUGHOUT MY work on the three editions of *Songs and Slang of the British Soldier*, I was learning by trial and error. In this next stage, I continued to do the same, but with fewer and less serious errors. 'He who never makes mistakes makes nothing.' (Yes; I know that, in 1899, Edward John Phelps, who died a year later, said that 'A man who makes no mistakes does not usually make anything'. Egotistically, I prefer the modified form.)

Fairly often during my researching for *Songs and Slang*, I resorted to Francis Grose's pioneering and entertaining work – it was the first true dictionary of slang and cant, as opposed to cant, or the language of the underworld, alone – *A Classical Dictionary of the Vulgar Tongue*, 1785. I consulted it mostly in the third edition (1796), the last that Grose himself revised. Why Grose? Well, for years he served as a captain of militia. Moreover, he studied and wrote about military history. I thought that his selections and comments might be useful. They were. John Brophy was so much impressed with the nature and value of Captain Grose's dictionary that he urged me to edit and publish a reprint of the third edition with a biographical and descriptive essay and with notes on such words and phrases as seemed to require a gloss either expository or historical. So I looked into the matter and decided that the result could and should be both attractive to the general intelligent reader and perhaps of service to the student of language.

For the essay, I did only a modicum of research. Luckily, I knew my eighteenth-century English literature fairly well and therefore also knew exactly where to look for enough information about that tremendous character, Francis Grose (1731?–1791), to be able to contribute a worth-while account. Someone should write a biography of the man! Perhaps someone is doing precisely this. All I hope is that it's not a thesis-writer. To do Grose justice, one should be mature, know English social history intimately, have a better than average acquaintance with English language, above all in its slangy and dialectal aspects, and possess wit and humour and tolerance. Grose's *Dictionary of the Vulgar Tongue* isn't for puritans. He observed closely and patiently, both for that book and for *A Provincial Glossary*. His researches for the latter took him over much of England. For a rather different purpose (topographical) he went to Scotland, where he met and made friends with Robert Burns; he is the object of Burns's famous remark – 'A chield's amang you taking notes, And, faith, he'll prent it' – and the dedicatee of the still more famous 'Tam o' Shanter'. The evenings those two passed together must have been memorable for wine and wit, but unfortunately nobody has printed notes of them. I suspect that neither Robert nor Francis, much less any of their quite sturdy compotators, retained a sufficiently clear head to be able to present a connected or even a coherent account of the ribald jests, the bibulous epigrams, the Rabelaisian stories.

My notes to the terms comprising the dictionary part of Grose's *Vulgar Tongue* were, in the main, brief and always pertinent. I wasn't trying to show what a clever or learned fellow I was, for I neither wish to be clever nor think of myself as learned. Already interested in slang and knowing something of cant, I soon noticed that a third field of linguistic knowledge would yield a wealth of matter germane to the task of annotating Grose: that of English dialect. Now, I don't pretend to know much about English dialect; in 1930–31, I knew still less. I therefore leaned heavily upon Joseph Wright's superb *English Dialect Dictionary*: painfully aware of my ignorance, I consulted 'Wright' whenever I was in doubt, and usually I checked by *The O.E.D.* In short, I did a much better job than, probably, I should have done had I been a good dialect scholar. If one is pretty good at a subject, one tends to miss things merely because one tends either to take them for granted or not even to think of them: starting from scratch, I exercised a very special care to miss nothing – well, very little – relevant to my purpose. (Better than alert and conscientious ignorance, better than a tolerable store of knowledge, is, of course, a thorough knowledge. Yet a thorough knowledge may, in its turn, result in dangerous assumptions and prejudices. 'But that is another story.') Looking back on my first serious piece of admittedly secondary lexicography, I find very little that I should wish to alter and remarkably little that could fittingly and profitably be augmented. That edition has been out of print since 1948 and cannot be bought under three or four times its original price.

But I have received so many complaints about this

lamentable state of affairs that, early in 1962, I finally yielded to my friends and their secret ally: I 'broke down' and decided to reissue my edition exactly as it stood in its original, except that fifteen-or-so slight errors ('literals') have been silently amended and that a brief note occurs at the head of my preface. The new edition is unlimited and, comparatively, a good deal cheaper than that of 1931. An unlimited edition is necessary, for the original appeared during the truly hard times of the Economic Depression of the early 1930's and, except in a very few isolated copies, did not reach the United States at all and hardly penetrated to the Dominions and elsewhere abroad. At last 'Grose' gets the opportunity he deserves.

During 1931–32 I published, in the weeklies, a number of articles dealing with such popular aspects of language as slang words and catch-phrases. Colonel F. C. C. Egerton, at that time the Chief Editor for Messrs George Routledge & Sons, read some of them, invited me to call on him and suggested that I should write a history and a study of slang. This I agreed to do. The book came out in September 1933. I mention it here because, after the main part, I appended three small glossaries, with entries brief and terse, yet precise and informative: English slang, American slang, Australian slang. Although unambitious, these glossaries yet achieved original lexicography; not a kind of lexicography suitable for all purposes; frankly inadequate to and horribly incongruous with the scope and nature of the usual straight-forward dictionary-making of such great works as *The O.E.D.* or *Webster's*; nevertheless, well adapted (I believe) to the needs of certain subjects I should be undertaking, off and on, during the next thirty years or so. It is a method I have modified and varied, improved and matured. Sometimes I have used this method only; sometimes, as in *Origins*, I have combined it with another; sometimes, as in *Usage and Abusage* and *Name into Word*, I have discarded it for other, more conventional, much more suitable, methods. A lexicographer needs to be supple and flexible in his methods and presentations; that is, if he wishes both to do the matter justice and to please the public – and, by the way, himself. Of these three considerations, the first is primary; the second, subsidiary; the third, idiosyncratic.

But no lexicographer should be permitted to indulge in principles and preferences without exemplifying the one and without justifying the other; not even when he desires to preserve a classical severity of form and an aesthetic smoothness of texture. A few quotations, however, will not irreparably damage the marmoreal surface of this urbane essay. (If the intrusion affronts you, it horripilates me.) The first and the second belong to the English section; the third to the American; the fourth to the Australian.

Fives. A foot: C17. Fingers = a fist (also *bunch of fives*): C19–20.

Flier. Anything unusually fast (–1850); a shoe: C17–19c. (gen. as *flyer*). Sense 1 was coll. by 1880, SE by 1900.

Ku-Klux, to. To join the Ku-Klux Klan (–1919); to act like a member thereof (–1920). The first Klan operated in 1866 and was a secret political organisation of the South.

Wowser. A strait-laced person. From *ca*. 1909. Coined by Norman Lindsay in a series of cartoons (*ca*. 1908).

In explanation: whereas 'c' means century, 'c' means cant; 'coll.', colloquial; 'gen.', generally, usually; *ca.*, everybody knows that one! The sign — before a date signifies that, recorded then, the term certainly goes further back. The examples show up a defect that was never repeated: in the terms of reference, only Proper Names, not all words, should be thus honoured with a capital; of the four examples, only *Ku-Klux* merits one. Formerly, as in *The O.E.D.*, capitals introduced every such key-word. I had followed that august exemplar. But in *A Dictionary of Slang*, on which I began to work in 1933, I discarded the unnecessary capitals; and that great recension of *Webster's New International Dictionary of the English Language* which appeared, as the second edition, in 1934, likewise employed capitals for Proper Names only. 'It should be clear to even the meanest intelligence' that the unnecessary use of capitals may easily lead to ambiguity or, at the least, to discomfort and resentment – 'the little something not quite right'. There you have one minor instance of the hundreds of problems constantly demanding a decision: and it is fatally easy to decide wrongly, sometimes for reasons convincing enough at the time.

IV: THE PROBLEM OF ALPHABETICAL ORDER

ON READING the proofs of *Slang Today and Yesterday*, Colonel Egerton must have conferred with the directors of Messrs George Routledge & Sons and applied his eloquence and charm with good effect, for in May or early June, 1933, I was invited by that excellent firm to write – not merely to compile – *A Dictionary of Slang and Unconventional English*. The two years stipulated by the contract had, by mutual consent, to be extended to three: and how I worked during those three years on the dictionary and during the next seven months on the proofs (slips or galleys, then pages)! I swore that I'd never again 'slave' like that; and yet, some years later, I 'slaved' even harder at *Origins*. That's what happens when one is engaged upon a large and fascinating piece of work. (Fascinating to the 'slave', I mean.) Unless one is a hack, adapting someone else's dictionary, lexicography is hard work; the conscientious lexicographer, if he has a passion for his subject, adds to the strain by doing more than, strictly, he needs to do, not so much because he wishes to perpetrate a supererogation as because he must. We hear of the compulsions of the creative writer – the poet and the dramatist, the novelist or the short-story practitioner. Those are genuine compulsions; the results, genuinely creative.

Yet the true scholar also has his compulsions: and his results may, in a different mode, be almost as creative as those of the other wielders of words. But enough of that – for the present, anyway.

As soon as I began to ponder the method, the technique, of writing *A Dictionary of Slang and Unconventional English* (or *D.S.U.E.*, as it is often called nowadays), I found that I had to solve problems of demarcation and classification and arrangement: what was, and what was not, eligible to figure in these august pages; to increase the value of the book, a classification into slang proper, colloquialism, catch-phrases (frequently difficult to distinguish from proverbial sayings) – and, at the very bottom of the social scale, vulgarisms on the one hand and, on the other, cant or the language of the under-world; and the arrangement, both that of senses within any given entry and that which is known as alphabetical order.

Alphabetical order? 'But surely,' the philistine exclaims, 'there is only one alphabetical order? Why mention the subject at all? We don't need to learn the A B C; we know it.' Many scholars not concerned with language, and even many non-lexicographical philologists, if they have not thought of the matter (after all, why should they?), are either totally unaware or, at best, very hazily aware, of the fact that there are two main alphabetical systems, with a third – combining the other two – employed by those humanitarians who do not wish either to carry logic to an absurdity or, like a house-proud woman, to pursue an ideal of perfection to the point where everyone else is discomforted and discomfited. Lexicography is not an abstraction, devised and practised for the delight of lexicographers. 'The operation was brilliantly

39

successful.' – 'And how is the patient?' – 'Oh, unfortunately he died, poor fellow.' That sort of thing simply won't do in lexicography. Even the 'perfect' alphabetical order has, on occasion, to be 'bent' a little to suit the customer's convenience.

The words that go to form the vocabulary of a language are much less tractable and malleable than most people seem to realize; even the words forming a specialist or sectional dictionary, as, for instance, of slang, can show themselves infuriatingly intractable. The two principal reasons for such unexpected recalcitrance are these: words aren't the only units of a language, for there are also phrasal verbs, phrasal prepositions, phrasal adverbs and adjectives, in addition to the phrases formed by metaphors and similes and idioms; and especially there are compound adjectives and nouns (and even verbs) as well as simples. All compounds have, at least potentially, three stages. At first they consist of two (or more) separate words, still regarded as two or more entities; thus, *lower class*, a noun used as an adjective. Then they are linked by means of a hyphen; *lower-class*, adjective. Finally they become one word, written 'solid'; *lowerclass*, adjective. (The preference of most Britons and many Americans for *lower-class* to *lowerclass* springs partly from habit and partly from aesthetic considerations and partly for reasons of convenience. Let us not quibble about aspects irrelevant here.)

The compromise method being, for a moment or two, deferred until we can clearly see which two systems the compromise is between, we have to consider the 'absolute', as it is usually known, or 'logical'; and the 'something before nothing' – the predominant name – or 'sensible'. Both 'logical', so much less logical than it may seem, and 'sensible', yet not always nor necessarily the best, are question-begging terms; yet, in so delicate a decision, so subtle an arrangement, it is difficult to avoid the begging of questions. For some dictionaries, the 'absolute' is probably the best; for others, the 'something-before-nothing'; for yet others, few but very important, some compromise is advisable, although it may not be indispensable.

The third method – 'the compromise' – arose because we human beings are not yet gods and are hindered and held back by imperfect memories and imperfect intellects. This method, in one or other of the varieties determined by circumstance, has therefore much to commend it.

The second method – 'something before nothing' – is perhaps the most satisfying, if considered at the psychological and aesthetic levels and judged by psychological and aesthetic criteria; yet because of compounds, it too has occasionally to be humanized by recourse to compromise.

The first method – 'the absolute' – cannot be faulted on grounds of either logic or methodology or economy. It never necessitates a repetition. Yet, because of its very perfection, it is the best only for a non-exclusive, hence a huge, dictionary; it makes no allowance for human imperfections and frailties.

The preceding trio of paragraphs may, to the carping and the querulous, look dangerously like a dramatic trick or a narrative 'gimmick': a contrivance of suspense. Those paragraphs are, in the fact, something very much less artful, for they aim only at an atmospheric adumbration; they amount to a genial hint that, thus forewarned, the layman is forearmed against the tedium that can so easily result from a consideration of what, to him, appears theoretical and is, in reality and practice, a set of devices designed to introduce clarity into obscurity, a light into darkness, a bulwark against chaos and despair. If anyone should think, 'This is rhetorical exaggeration,' he thereby condemns himself as both ignorant and stupid, and also as hopelessly imperceptive and insensitive. Lexicography is an art vastly more complex and difficult and arduous than the lay consulters of dictionaries can possibly imagine. Lexicographers, you may be sure, wish it were otherwise.

The 'absolute' order, provided that it be prosecuted 'to the letter' and then mitigated by additions or insertions wherever the consulter's convenience is involved, is theoretically the best order of all; yet such modification would, of course, remove it from the first to the third, or 'compromise', group. The genuine or 'one-hundred-per-cent.' absolute order has never been followed, even in that great work which professes to have adopted the system. *Webster's New International Dictionary* has gone the closest to observing 'the absolute alphabetical order'. (The ensuing 'specimen section' has been based upon – indeed taken from – that scrupulous recension which appeared in 1934 as the Second Edition.) Not only has it apparently done so; it has also really done so – in the main.

Before I take a difficult example and analyse it, let me give an easy one, first in absolute order, then in 'something before nothing'. (As it's an easy example, there is no need for compromise; and, to be a valid, not a contrived, example, it must come from a small dictionary.)

SET, v., to place, to put, etc. Its various senses. Followed, within the same entry, by *set*, adjective, and *set*, noun, with their various senses. Then, still within the entry: the compound nouns, as *set-back*; a compound adjective; the derivatives *setter*, with its off-shoots, and *setting*; then, in one alphabetical list, both the phrasal verbs, beginning with *set about*, and the true phrases, *set at naught – set eyes on – set one's teeth – set speech* – etc.

That main entry, which, even in this excellent general-purpose smallish dictionary (*Chambers's Twentieth Century Dictionary*), is dauntingly large, is followed by SETA, SETON, SETTEE (two distinct words), SETTER and SETTING referred to SET, the technical verb SETTER, SETTLE, noun and verb (-MENT, -R, etc.) – SETWALL (or SETUALE) – SEVEN . . .

But, you'll notice, there are no separate entries, even of cross-reference, either for such a compound as *set-back*, now often written *setback*, or for phrases of any kind. Then why are SETTER and SETTING cross-referenced? Clearly, they represent a compromise – a concession to those consulters who may not immediately connect them with SET.

And if this happens in a smallish dictionary, what's going to happen in a large, especially in a vast, one? The 'defect' – if that be the right word – should not be blamed on the particular dictionary: as I've said, it's a very good piece of work. I could take any other small or smallish dictionary and display similar 'defects': 'defects' caused by the very nature of the English language – by the very nature of any analytical language. (A Greek or a Latin dictionary is much easier to handle.)

That *Chambers's Twentieth Century* specimen is fundamentally and predominantly an example of 'something

before nothing': all SET senses and compounds and phrases
are disposed of before SETA, SETON, etc., are treated.

The 'absolute' arrangement of those words and phrases
would run something like this; only 'something like this',
for I do not include every single compound and phrase.

> SET, v., n., adj. – or separated into SET, adj. –
> SET, n. – SET, v. (or some other order)
>
> SETA
>
> SET ABOUT
>
> SET AGAINST
>
> SET APART
>
> SET ASIDE
>
> SET AT NAUGHT
>
> SET BACK and SETBACK
>
> SET BY (to put aside)
>
> SET DOWN
>
> SET EYES ON
>
> SET FIRE TO
>
> SET FORTH
>
> SET IN
>
> SET OFF
>
> SET ON (to incite)
>
> SETON (thread)
>
> SET PIECE
>
> SET SPEECH
>
> SETTEE (1)
>
> SETTEE (2)
>
> SETTER
>
> SET TERMS

SETTING

SETTLE (1), noun

SETTLE (2), verb; SETTLEMENT, SETTLER, etc.

SET UP, v., and SET-UP (or SETUP), n.

SET UPON (to attack)

SETWALL

SEVEN

That, an example of the 'absolute alphabetical order', has much to commend it: the consulter will be able to find immediately any word, whether simple or compound or direct derivative, and any phrase whatsoever. Yet, if he did not know that this order governed the arrangement or did not fully realize its implications, he might be brought up short and feel perplexed and perhaps resentful. An 'absolute' lexicographer might well hesitate; and, hesitating, be not lost but sane; he would probably arrange the phrasal verbs and the phrases in one alphabetical order immediately after the verb – and *not* repeat them; such a compound noun as SET-UP (or SETUP) would cause him a headache, nor would it be the only one. The 'absolute' order has ceased to be absolute: a concession has been made to good sense and to semantic congruity and unity. Yet if the lexicographer carries semantic congruity – senses following senses in what seems a natural order – much further, he will be sacrificing convenience.

'That's all very well,' an irritated reader may understandably exclaim, 'but what would *you* do about it? Can you suggest a method that will preserve both the consulter's convenience and a degree of congruity and commonsense?' That's a good question.

45

First of all, I should hope to make it clear that every consulter of any dictionary of the words and phrases forming the
vocabulary of an analytical language (English, French, German, Spanish, Italian, etc.) must bear in mind the irrefutable
and inescapable fact that, in this matter of alphabetical order,
perfection is impossible. Secondly, I should compromise;
yet, for the compromise to be appreciated or even under-
stood, the consulter should be induced to read the preliminary
'Note on Arrangement' – if there is one. If the dictionary is
either small or specialist, there may be no need for a 'Note'.

The compromise would take the form of 'something
before nothing', with an occasional repetition made for the
sake of convenience: a modified 'something-before-nothing'.
Theorizing is here of little use. This is how, if I were confronted with the task of editing the *Chambers's* material, I
should do it; but, both that lexicographer and I preferring a
'something-before-nothing' to an 'absolute' arrangement,
we should differ only in details.

SET (1), adjective
    set back, recessed
SET (2), noun
    set-back or *setback*, a reverse
    set-down, a rebuff
    set-off, a claim offsetting another claim
    set-out, a display
    set-to, a bout of fisticuffs, a momentary
        quarrel
    set-up or *setup*, an arrangement
SET (3), verb

All the phrasal verbs and the full phrases arranged in one alphabetical order and, as for the noun, indented and italicized, thus:

set about
set against
set apart
set aside
set at naught
set back, to check, etc.
. . . .
set eyes on
. . . .
set little, or *much, store by*
. . . .
set one's heart on
set one's teeth
. . . .
set piece
. . . .
set terms
set to (to begin a meal, etc.)
. . . .
set up ('That'll set you up')
set upon

SETA
SET-BACK or SETBACK. See SET (2)
SET-DOWN. See SET (2)
SET-OFF. See SET (2)

47

(But, if economy were necessary:
  SET-BACK, SET-DOWN, SET-OFF. See SET (2))
SETON
SET-OUT. See SET (2)
SETTEE (1), the seat
SETTEE (2), the sailing-ship
SETTER (1), noun
SETTER (2), verb
SETTING, noun
SETTLE (1), noun (a long bench with a high
  back)
SETTLE (2), verb, with its derivatives, SETTLE-
  MENT, SETTLER, SETTLING-DAY, etc.
SET-TO. See SET (2)
SET-UP. See SET (2)

The critical consulter will inevitably and most properly ask, 'But if the compound nouns receive the honour of a cross-reference, why not the phrasal verbs and the full phrases?' My answer would be, 'Because they immediately precede the new series (beginning with *seta*) and because they are so very numerous that repetition would amount to one of the "larger lunacies" and because, unlike the compound nouns, they are not written "solid" as one word, the general rule for nouns in American English (witness *setback*, *setdown*, *setoff*, *setout*, *setup*, etc.) and a practice increasingly common elsewhere in English.' If the critical fellow then objected, 'That isn't very logical, is it?' – I should reply, 'If the arrangement of any large dictionary were entirely logical, as opposed to part-logical, part-sensible, and to part-absolute, part-convenient, you would probably lose your way in it'. Compromise is not merely advisable, often it is necessary and – except to fanatics – unavoidable.

In the *Chambers* entry, I suppressed one item. The phrase *dead set*, as in 'to make a *dead set* against someone', occurs, within the main SET entry, at the beginning of the list of phrases and is disposed of in the instruction, 'see DEAD-SET'. This is the more usual of the two main techniques, the other being to list the phrase as SET, DEAD, and to place SET, DEAD, immediately after the last of the simple SET entries. The latter is the practice I adopted in *A Dictionary of Slang*, where '*have* (a person) *set*' appears as 'SET, *have* (a person)' and comes next after SET, DEAD. All such phrases naturally – in the 'something before nothing' system – precede all such phrases as *set about, set at naught*, . . . *set upon*.

Perhaps that comparatively simple cluster of SET entries and the reasonably compact indication of the three best ways of dealing with the cluster as a whole, hence with its distinct parts, will have adequately conveyed to the layman the (I hope) salutary fact that non-imitative lexicography requires unceasing care, unflagging awareness, unwearying alertness – and a very clear head. Like other men, lexicographers are, despite a deplorably widespread belief to the contrary, only human; they occasionally nod drowsily and 'drop a (verbal) brick'; and, like the legendary pianist in a Wild West saloon, they should not be shot, but merely forgiven.

After that relatively simple exemplification of alphabetical order, a rather more advanced exposition will be nonchalantly taken in their stride by all intelligent readers: and anyone who reads this little book stands self-condemned as intelligent and properly inquisitive. But I'll try to render the exposition acceptable by continuing with SET. This time, I shall analyse the entries in *Webster's New International* (in its ever to be cherished recension of 1934) and *The Shorter Oxford Dictionary* (edition of 1956) and *A Dictionary of Slang* (1961 edition): for treatments respectively 'absolute' or, rather, predominantly so – 'something before nothing' – 'compromise'. This time, however, I shall make the treatment as mercifully brief as possible; I certainly don't want my patient readers to die from sheer boredom.

Webster deals with our SET thus: verb, adjective, noun. The verb, defined in its multiple senses, is followed by all the phrases, the phrasal verbs (*set about*, *set by*, etc.) merged with the true phrases in one continuous 'absolute' alphabetical order, the final *set up one's pipes* coming next after *set upon*. The adjective – strictly, the past-participial adjective – is shrewdly defined; its use in combination (*close-set*, *thickset*) receives an immediately following separate entry. The noun is then defined in detail.

All that is sufficiently obvious. But what happens next? The ensuing SET entries are these:

> SET, a standard of value
> SET, a dialectal variant of 'to *sit*'
> SETA and its derivatives
> SETBACK
> SET BAR
> SETBOLT

SET BOOK

SET CHISEL

SETDOWN (British *set-down*)

SETEBOS

SET–FAIR

SET GAUGE

SET GUN

SETH

SETH

SET HAMMER

SET-HANDS and a derivative

SETHEAD

SETH GREEN

SETHIAN – SETHIC – SETHITE

SET HOOK

SETI–

SETIBO

SETIFERA

SET–IN

SETLINE

SET NUT

SET OF ASSOCIATED ELEMENTS

SET OF DAY

SET OF EXCHANGE

SETOFF (British *set-off*)

SET OF THREADS

SETON, n. (1)

SETON, v.

SETON, n. (2)

SETOPHAGA

SETOSE – SETOUS

SETOUT (British *set-out*)

SETOVER (British *set-over*)

SET PIECE

SET PIN

SET POINT

SET POT

SETSCREW (British *set screw* or *set-screw*)

SETSMAN

SET SQUARE

SET-STITCHED

SETT – three distinct nouns

SETTECENTO

SETTEE – two distinct nouns

SETTEE BED

SET TEMPER

SETTER – two distinct nouns

SETTER, verb

SETTER-FORTH

SETTERGRASS

SETTER-IN

SETTER-ON

SETTER-OUT

SETTER-TO

SETTER-UP

SETTERWORT

SETTIMA, SETTIMO

SETTING

SETTING BLOCK or BOARD and some eighteen
other *setting* combinations

SETTLE, noun (the long, wooden, high-backed seat)

SETTLE, verb and ten derivative ph ases, e.g.
SETTLE ACCOUNTS

SETTLE, n. (2) – a physical settling

SETTLEABLE

SETTLE BED

SETTLE-BENCH

SETTLE-BRAIN

SETTLED, adjective, and six dependent combinations

SETTLEMENT and four combinations

SETTLER

SETTLER'S-CLOCK

SETTLER'S MATCHES

SETTLER'S TWINE

SETTLING, participial adjective and verbal noun; with four dependants

SETTLOR

SET-TO

SETTSMAN

SET TUB

SETULA and SETULE

SETULIFORM

SETULOSE and SETULOUS

SETUP (British *set-up*), n.

SET UP, adj.

SETWALL (which has nothing to do with SET)

SETWISE

SETWORK

SEUGH

SEVEN

etc.

The list, one notices, is itself in 'absolute' order – except that it omits both the phrasal verbs and the true phrases based upon the verb *set*, all of which have appeared immediately after SET (verb) and have thus followed, not the 'absolute' but the 'something-before-nothing' principle. Had the 'absolute' principle been rigidly adhered to, every word, whether simple or compound, and every phrase of any sort would have been displayed in one continuous and exceptionless order: thus would a kind of doctrinaire logic and systematic purity have been preserved – to the detriment of good sense and semantic congruity.

How, then, does the treatment in *The Shorter Oxford English Dictionary* differ from that in *Webster*? Compressed and rationalized as far as it is possible to go without obscuring the argument ('I labour to be brief and I become obscure'), the SET material in *The S.O.E.D.* is exhibited in this engagingly intelligent manner*:

SET, noun (1), corresponding to the verb

SET, n. (2), group of persons, collection of things

SET, verb, scrupulously and subtly defined under ten heads; at the end of each head, the relevant phrases or proverbs. After the

* I have changed all unnecessary initial capitals to small letters.

tenth sense: 'combinations' (phrasal verbs) with prepositions (*set about*, etc.) and – a very long list – with adverbs (*set afloat*, etc.)

SET, participial adjective, with the relevant 'combinations' (*set dance*, etc.)

SET-, the combining-form of the v. *set*

SETA, followed by SETACEOUS

SET-BACK

SET-DOWN

SETI-, combining-form of SETA

SETNESS

SET-OFF

SETON

SETOSE

SET-OUT

SETT

SETTEE (1) and SETTEE (2)

SETTER and, within the entry, its combinations

SETTERWORT

SETTING, noun and its 'combinations'

SETTING DOG

SETTLE, noun

SETTLE, verb, defined under six heads, with relevant phrases under each head

SETTLED, participial adjective

SETTLEMENT

SETTLER

SETTLING, noun, and a derivative

SETTLOR

SET-TO

SETULE

SETWALL

SÈVE

SEVEN

etc.

There you have a truly excellent example of 'something before nothing': everything is placed where the sense demands that it should be, and nothing is repeated; the principal meanings are followed immediately by the shades of meaning and by the phrases connected with those meanings and nuances: or, at least, all this has been so brilliantly achieved that one guiltily wonders, 'Why were the compound nouns *set-back*, *set-down*, *set-off*, *set-out* and *set-to* singled out for the special treatment of a separate entry?' Also, perhaps, 'Why have these nouns been separated from the corresponding phrasal verbs?' The answer, as I see it, is that they are sufficiently important to merit a separate entry. Moreover, you will probably have noticed that *Webster* does exactly the same thing, as you will certainly have noticed that neither dictionary repeats the phrasal verbs and that you must go looking for them at the verb SET.

Two facts emerge. Firstly, no alphabetical order is perfect. Even if every simple and compound word, every possible combination, every phrase of every sort, every proverb and proverbial saying, were placed in the literally 'absolute' order, there would still be problems arising from the 'Which is the key-word in "to *set at naught*" – *set* or *naught*?' class of question; the solution being the simple one of cross-reference. Secondly, the consulter of any large dictionary should study that preliminary section (if any) which tells him how to use the dictionary. *The O.E.D.* provides no such section, nor does *The S.O.E.D.*; Webster does, under the title 'Explanatory Notes'.

So do I in *A Dictionary of Slang and Unconventional English*, where, the material being vastly smaller in quantity, all I need to provide is a brief, perhaps a too brief, 'Note on Arrangement'. Yet various worthy persons have written to tell me that they could not find this word or that phrase. What they couldn't find was usually there, and in its right place; the complainers had omitted to read the 'Note'; but then, you can't help some people!

Perhaps the list of SET entries in *D.S.U.E.* will dispel a few remaining doubts. It cannot, of course, dispel all doubts, for reasons already laboured quite sufficiently in this tedious yet – by the honest lexicographer – unavoidable chapter. (The list is that of Volume I, the first edition revised. To incorporate the SET entries of the Supplement would merely confuse the issue yet further.)

SET, noun
SET, verb
SET, adjective
SET, DEAD
SET, HAVE (a person)
SET ABOUT
SET BACK
SET-DOWN
SET IN A CRACK
SET JEWELS

SET–ME–UP

SET–OUT

SET THE HARE'S HEAD . . .

SET THE SWEDE DOWN

SET–UP, noun

SET UP, verb

SET–UP, adjective

SET UP FOR, BE

SETACEOUS

SETS–OFF, –OUT, –TO

SETTA

SETTER

SETTER, CLOCK–

SETTING DOG

SETTLE

SETTLE (a person's) HASH

SETTLEMENT–IN–TAIL

SETTLER

SETTLER'S BIBLE, THE

SEVEN, ALL IN THE

The increasingly common practice among lexicographers engaged in any major work is to supply a set of hints on How to Use This Dictionary. They cannot, however, supply to would-be users either the intelligence to think of looking for such hints or the patience to read them very carefully. In small, still more in very small, dictionaries, such a key is hardly necessary: yet the proper and especially the effectual use of any dictionary whatsoever calls for the exercise of a modicum of average intelligence and of commonsense. And no matter how small the dictionary may be, there is always a list of abbreviations. Not to go to the slight trouble of assimilating that list is to ask for much greater trouble.

In the selfish ardours of intellectual abstraction, I have said nothing about an aspect of much greater interest to the general reader, however intelligent and tolerant he may be.

I could not begin to estimate how many times I have been asked, 'How on earth did you go about gathering the material for *A Dictionary of Slang*?' The better-informed have usually added a number of sensible remarks which might be compounded and summarized in some such way as this: 'After all, the problem is quite different from that which faced the editors of *The O.E.D.* or *Webster*. They examined thousands of books and periodicals and presumably they depended to some extent upon oral tradition. Also, they had scores – probably hundreds – of helpers; one rather supposes that such helpers are still available to them. But you are, for the present century, dealing with a vast body of material of which rather a lot, surely, isn't available in the usual way.'

First of all, I'd like to make it clear that, after material has been collected, it needs to be sifted; then collated; finally, edited – a term that veils an entire complex of operations. Secondly, any such undertaking as *The O.E.D.* or *Webster's* must be carried out by a large team. Thirdly, that the 'lone wolf' is less lonely than, to the uninformed, he may seem. Fourthly, this particular 'lone wolf' has enjoyed advantages denied to the majority of such creatures: advantages afforded partly by environment and circumstance, partly by pre-dilection and addiction.

'That's all very well. That's "fine, wide and handsome". But could we,' asks an irritated consulter of dictionaries, 'could we, please, "cut the cackle and come to the 'osses"? Could we "get down to cases"? We wish to know how you went about gathering and checking the material for *D.S.U.E.*, not how other lexicographers might have done it nor even how they think *you* should have done it. You wrote it, not they – nor do we think it at all likely that any one of them *could* have written it.'

Ah, well! On your own heads . . .

I did not come to the task a virgin. Already, you will remember, I had been concerned with *Songs and Slang of the British Soldier*; I had published a number of articles on slang and colloquialism; I had edited Grose's *Vulgar Tongue*; I had just finished studying the entire field of slang and its related subjects in order to write *Slang Today and Yesterday*. So much for a tolerable preliminary knowledge of the subject and so much for some slight experience of technique. No less important, however, was the fact that the publication of those three books and of those articles had brought me many acquaintances, several of whom became good friends and a few of whom became faithful correspondents over periods varying from a couple of years (people die or are either submerged or immersed) to thirty or more. Then there were others: people I met, people who met me: and these others communicated by word of mouth.

'Oh! One presumes that any and every writer, especially upon such a subject as English, receives such communications and perhaps goes so far as to maintain such contacts. But what *sort* of person got into touch with you? And for what *reason* – or *reasons*?'

All sorts of persons communicated with me: 'dons' and dustmen; school teachers and schoolboys, but not, if I remember correctly, schoolgirls; butchers and bakers – but no candlestick makers; sailors and soldiers and airmen; games-players and gamesters; Civil Servants and domestic servants; railwaymen and busmen and tram-drivers; huntsmen and motorists; actors and authors, doctors and divines; journalists and publicity men (and women); social workers and prison warders; beggars and tramps; petty crooks and one or two (I suspected) major criminals; sheep farmers and sheep shearers; cattlemen and commercial travellers; shopmen and clubmen. You name them; I got them. Whereas some could hardly write, others wrote almost too well, or was it rather too much? Often those who wrote most, told me least. A very few 'tried it on', either by making up words and phrases or by pretending they meant something quite different: they forgot that I have myself 'been around' and that I could, and would, check their fantasies. I often wish that I had kept all those letters. Clearly, I couldn't. There were far, far too many of them. I own a small house, not a warehouse.

The reasons these good people had for helping me can, in the last resort, be reduced to three. The majority wished to help, and that's all there was to it, for most people are helpful; a few hoped to see their names in print; a very few, I believe, wished to prove how much they knew about the subject – in brief, to 'show off'. Among scholars and among all kinds of writers, some – indeed, the greater part – were attracted by the project itself and, like the general majority, wished to contribute, with no thought of gain and, apart from an occasional publicity-hunter, with no desire to be named. I did not name all my correspondents; some of them expressly asked not to be named. But, whenever I could, I named all those who had contributed considerably or otherwise notably.

Although I shouldn't need to say this, I instituted a vast number of oral and scriptural inquiries and received almost no rude answers. I read a vast number of books and periodicals, including many sources that had apparently eluded all my predecessors. I had, moreover, the great good fortune to be allowed, by my publishers, to use, as freely as I desired, a work that was entirely their property: Farmer & Henley's *Slang and Its Analogues* (seven volumes, 1890–1904) – the relevant entries of which, in fact, I adopted as an expansible framework. I owe a great deal to that work and I have never tried to minimize the debt; nor do I wish to do so. On the other hand, even for the period up to (say) 1890, I have dealt far more richly and, above all, far more pertinently with the subject.

V: TRIFLES

✳✳✳

BY 'TRIFLES' I mean no more than that, compared with the dictionaries of slang and cant and etymology, the six books treated in this chapter are small; one or two, very small indeed. Three of them, moreover, are already out of print; a fourth, I hope, soon will be; and of only one do I regret the passage, for, of all six, it was, lexicographically, the best piece of work and, generally, the most readable and entertaining. 'But, there you are, that's the way things go' or, in Elizabethan English, ' 'Tis a mad world, my masters'.

The first to appear, and probably the last to remain, in print, was *Name This Child*, a dictionary of given or Christian Names, British and American. 'Christian names' is the usual British term, 'given names', the usual American, although 'Christian name' is far commoner in the United States than 'given name' is in Britain. I was invited by that delightful essayist, E. V. Lucas (1868–1938), at that time the Managing Director of Messrs Methuen & Company, to 'do' a small book on the subject. Mr Lucas proposed the title, *Name This Child*. As a joke, I countered with *The Nameless Child*, which he rejected; yet, when he received the typescript, he wrote to ask whether I did not think *The Nameless Child* a more effective title; I gently reminded him that that title was my

63

'child' but that I preferred his original. He was an agreeable person, with a very keen sense of humour.

I wrote the book as, in part, a potboiler and as a refreshment, a light relief from my exciting and exhausting labours on *D.S.U.E.* It came out in 1936 and had no pretensions to scholarship. In the second edition (1938), the worst errors disappeared. During the War, it went out of print. In 1951, Messrs Hamish Hamilton re-issued it in an improved edition, yet still essentially a 'bread-and-butter job'. But in 1945, the Oxford University Press had brought out Miss E. G. Withycombe's very much better *Oxford Dictionary of Christian Names* (second edition 1950), and so, when a few years later the opportunity occurred, the publisher and I decided to discard *Name This Child* in its then current form and to issue the book in a drastic abridgement at a price nobody else would sanely try to 'cut': the absurd sum of five shillings. Anyone who wants a very good, reasonably priced, book rightly goes for the Oxford publication, but anyone who wants a now passably good, very cheap one, goes for mine. Between us, we do rather tend to 'cream' the market. Anyway, I found the book fun to write, nor do I regret having written it.

During the fifteen months or so before my enlistment, early September 1940, in the King's Royal Rifles (Home Defence), I sought relief from work on *Underworld* by preparing two small books: *A New Testament Word-Book* and *A Dictionary of Clichés*, which appeared about a month after I became a Rifleman.

In the *Word-Book*, very properly based upon the Authorized Version or King James's Bible, I naturally confined myself to English words and phrases either obsolete or obsolescent. I treated them from both the literary and the linguistic angle, with frequent citations of the Greek original and of the Vulgate Latin. A slight book, it stood very little chance during the War years and soon afterwards it went to a remainder merchant; yet it did not entirely lack a certain merit of manner and presentation. Extremely few copies having reached America, *A New Testament Word-Book* is qualifying for the dubious distinction of rarity.

But *A Dictionary of Clichés* has a very different history, for it was conceived in jest, borne in ribaldry and born in merriment. As a joke, I proposed to the late Cecil Franklin, managing director of the house of Routledge, that I should prepare a 20,000-'worder' on the burning question, the *crambe repetita*, of clichés – a brief introductory essay and a not too solemn glossary of these contagious commonplaces of hurried or unthinking speech and of flabby writing; these mere counters of conversation and substitutes for thought; these facilities of the lazy and these godsends of the mediocre. Probably I had disliked the thought of an idea going to waste. Several months earlier, I had proposed to the Oxford University Press that I should write for them a Society for Pure English tract on clichés. But no unanimous opinion, let alone a generally accepted definition, could be attained at the Press; in self-defence, the 'selectors' had to say No. As compensation, they invited me to 'do' a tract on slang. I did it. I also approached Messrs Routledge about clichés.

What began as a jape ended as a not altogether unworthy book of 60,000 words or so. Whereas the introduction had remained brief, the glossary ran away with me, the field turning out to be much richer than I had suspected. Admittedly I went along with the tide, and I'm now glad that I acted so weak-mindedly. The book is all the better for being much larger than I had originally intended, all the more so that I was thus enabled to include a certain number of predominantly American clichés. The work has been revised and very slightly enlarged; it has also had the audacity to go into six or seven printings. As a particularly horrible warning, it is a useful and almost readable book; it is also and unashamedly a light-weight. For me it has never quite lost its initial unreality and its preliminary irreverence: although I had not gone to scoff and remained to pray, I had gone to scoff and remained to wonder.

Throughout 1941 I was in the Army and constantly being exasperated by the many new abbreviations impeding an immediate understanding of much that I was obliged to read and forced to understand. Inevitably it occurred to me that I should be helping not only myself but numerous other victims of this martial – or, rather, of this official – mania if I were to compile a short and practical guide. Almost as inevitably I decided that servicemen might be grateful if I included the more important of the ordinary or 'civilian' abbreviations. During my own civilian interlude of ten months or so (late January-very early December, 1942) I completed this minor work and saw it appear in January 1943, by which time I was in the RAF. In the second edition, many Air Force terms were added; in the third, the too few Naval terms mounted to something like respectability. But the book has not been revised and enlarged since 1949, and I shall be glad when it goes out of print, for two reasons:

there are more urgent, more attractive, things for me to do; and there have, since 1949, appeared two dictionaries superior to mine, the one for British abbreviations, the other for the entire English-speaking world. Although I have become bored with this utilitarian work, I did, while I was assembling and compiling it, prevent it from being hopelessly mechanical by allowing myself, perhaps half a dozen times, to expatiate or to comment, as at

'*ADC*. Aide-de-Camp. That officer who acts as courier and secretary to a general. He must be affable, courteous, and very, very tactful; ready-witted and of an infinite resource; immaculately attired.'

While I was still in the RAF, I kept my hand in by writing – this time, writing, not merely compiling – *A Dictionary of RAF Slang*, which appeared late in the January of 1945. It was only a very small book, with a short essay preceding the glossary. Like every other book ever published, it has its faults; like every other reference book, its inaccuracies – at least in the first edition. My *RAF Slang* never got beyond its first edition of 5,000 copies, exhausted before the year was out. Paper was short; books far more important had to be published.

I've always thought well of this little book, written with affection for 'the youngest Service' and in admiration for the fighter and bomber crews; as a whole, rather well done, I believe. That it should so soon have gone out of print, however, ceased to irk me when, in 1947, I edited and, in 1948, saw appear *A Dictionary of Forces' Slang*, 1939–1945, to which, not unnaturally, I contributed the Air Force entries. I planned the book very simply, with the result that the collation of material was much less wearisome than it usually is in such collaborative undertakings. I was doubly fortunate in being able to enlist the help of two of my friends, who, what is more, were 'just the men for the job'.

Indeed, it was from one of these two friends that, indirectly, I got the idea. Wilfred Granville had, just after the War, submitted to my approval a glossary of the Navy's slang of the Second World War. Although it was a good piece of work, two or three publishers rejected it. It dawned on me that, on the basis of his typescript and, if revised and enlarged, my out-of-print book, we had the makings of a 'collective effort': I had only to persuade someone to prepare an Army glossary, and there we were! The work of collation and then of editing took a little time, but at least it was a straight-forward task. For the Army slang, I invited Frank Roberts, a master at Cotton College in North Staffordshire. As a former student, and a lifelong disciple, of Ernest Weekley's, he had the training, and as an Artillery officer with friends in the other arms of the Service, he had the knowledge. I wrote a short introduction. This was, in all respects, a thoroughly competent piece of work, accurate and instructive and tolerably comprehensive; and no one found the book dull. But it appeared some years too soon and did not meet with the success it deserved. It failed to go into a second edition, and when, three or four years after publication, the last copy was sold, the publishers hardly felt compelled to reprint.

For me, of course, *Forces' Slang* held a particular interest. John Brophy and I had dealt with the First World War, and now Wilfred Granville and Frank Roberts and I had taken care of the Second World War. Yet I was not one of those who, the day after either war broke out, 'began to write a history of it' – as several famous writers were accused of doing. Nor had *A Dictionary of RAF Slang* been a merely topical book, in that my motive was not that of wishing to 'cash in' but that of wishing to 'shoot these words on the wing' – while I was still living them and they were living things.

VI: MIDDLE-WEIGHTS

In 1938, I suggested to the publishers of *A Dictionary of Slang* that I should write a book on good English and bad, under the title of *Usage and Abusage*. They were suitably horrified. They very firmly told me that anyone daring to compete with Henry Watson Fowler's *Modern English Usage* was thereby proposing to commit suicide and that they would be no party to what, after all, was a criminal offence. I very gently told them that I wasn't proposing to do anything quite so fatuous and that my book, written at a much less august level and in a rather less Augustan manner, would serve as a complement and a supplement to 'Fowler'. I also reminded them that M.E.U., although doubtless revised for printers' and other minor errors, had never been enlarged or brought up to date, and that, with its author dead, it couldn't be. But no! They would not have it at any price. I must say that I don't for a moment blame them: from their angle, they were so right that I had to suppress a feeling of guilt as having mentioned anything so iconoclastic.

There are, however, two sides to every book – the publisher's and the author's. As a professional writer, I still thought that there was room for such a modest work as *Usage and Abusage*, and so I put the idea up to Hamish

Hamilton, who lost no appreciable time in accepting it. During 1938 and 1939 – or, rather, at odd moments, and occasionally for relief from a certain long and arduous task – I worked on U. & A., as the irreverent call it. At the very beginning of 1940, I delivered the typescript.

Owing to shortage of paper, the book did not get itself published in Britain until the Spring of 1947. In the United States, it came out in 1942; there it duly exhausted three editions, whereupon, for some odd reason, the American publishers decided that they would not be continuing to publish *Usage and Abusage*. One can only suppose that they lost interest. The book is still quite easily obtainable in America: and that's a very good thing, because it is no less advisable for educated Americans to acquaint themselves with British usage than it is for literate Britons to at least be able to recognize an American usage when they meet one.

Such a book as this of mine could be described as back-door or, at best, side-door lexicography. The multiple subjects and aspects are arranged in alphabetical order, with a considerable number of cross-references to the main articles. Lexicographically, this was an easy task. But, as a whole, *Usage and Abusage* did not prove to be an easy book to write and I wasn't satisfied with the way it turned out. All the same, there's no denying that it has, to a moderate extent, 'caught on'. Four editions appeared within a few years and, within a decade of its British publication, the publisher and I decided to revise it, enlarge it, and bring it up to date. This I did, without detriment to the sales, all the more so because I pruned away much material that, interesting enough, was largely irrelevant. So far, it has been one of my three best sellers, the other two being *A Dictionary of Slang* and *Origins*. But U. & A. is, I think, inferior to those two. I also happen to think it a pretty useful book and a practical book, a book that, because of its arrangement in the form of a dictionary, is easy to consult and to use. The mingling of specific words and phrases with subjects has always struck me as being strange lexicographical practice. Yet, in any such book as this, it is not only customary, but unavoidable. Nevertheless, one has to resist the temptation – a very strong temptation – either to increase the spatial discrepancy between entries dealing with a specific abuse and those involving an entire subject by shortening the former still further and by lengthening the articles, or, on the other hand, to reduce the discrepancy by elaborating the brevities and by compacting the leisurelies.

The publisher went further. He persuaded me to prepare a much smaller work, to be called *The Concise Usage and Abusage*. He felt that such a book was desirable, especially because the much lower price would render it available to a much larger public and because, in a shorter form, with all abstruse or difficult matter excluded, it would better serve the purposes of schools in general. The Sixth Forms of the best British schools could and would still use the major work, as also would undergraduates and writers and other serious students of English.

To some extent, the preparation of a concise form of any such book is 'mechanical'; to a much larger extent, it calls for great care and tact. What to leave in – what to cut out? But then, it's not merely a question of omitting certain entries and retaining others. Many of the articles one decides to retain have to be either shortened or, in other ways, modified; nor is the shortening done only by the simple removal of a quotation or two; no 'reduction' is – or, at least, should be – quite so easy as that! Often, too, there is a shift of emphasis, demanded either by the new public or by the new scope. I do not pretend that the work excited me, but it did constantly hold my attention and occasionally amuse me. Anyway, the sales would seem to have proved the publisher right (he usually is) and to have justified my work upon the project. Three large impressions within six years supply an argument not readily refuted, except by those who equate success to demerit.

The year 1947 witnessed the publication of another book that had long been delayed by the shortage of paper: *Shakespeare's Bawdy*. (This title, by the way, does not pun on 'Shakespeare is bawdy'; it was adopted as more euphonious than 'Shakespeare's Bawdry'.)

Like many other admirers of Shakespeare, I had for years resented that hypocrisy and that stupidity which descend upon otherwise intelligent persons when they come to discuss the bawdy element in his plays and poems. Either they tried to minimize it or they exaggerated it or they distorted by setting it in a false perspective. If it be true that to the pure all things are pure, it is equally true that to the dirty all things are dirty. The snigger is even more objectionable than the guffaw.

I wished to fulfil a dual purpose: to write a compact, meaty, short introduction on bawdry in Shakespeare, literary and psychological rather than linguistic – and psychological only in the fundamental sense, without recourse either to psychiatric or to ephemeral jargon; and to write rather than compile such a glossary of the bawdy words and phrases as would inform and satisfy the intelligent members of the general public and not entirely disappoint the specialist scholars; non-specialist students would, I knew, welcome the book. And any writer allowing himself to be irritated by the few carpers, envious ones, cannibals of the academic world, would be better employed in road-mending.

The essay – well, you might call it that – runs to some 15,000 words and is divided into six refreshingly unequal parts: Introductory; Non-sexual Bawdy; Homosexual; Sexual; General; Valedictory. Not even the index to the essay has escaped criticism, and yet even the index has been approved. The Glossary (50,000 words or so) is, for most readers, sufficiently comprehensive. I do not claim that it is all-inclusive. Apparently I have missed several words and phrases that, although not overtly bawdy or, if you prefer, are not bawdy in their denotations, are yet covertly so, their connotations and implications setting the matter beyond reasonable doubt. Besides indicating the references and usually quoting at least one passage, I clarified the meaning only if it were necessary to do so; mentioned parallels; provided etymologies, based mainly upon the excellent etymological matter in Wyld's *Universal English Dictionary*. I should have liked to quote a couple of entries, just to show the way – or, at least, one of the ways – in which a subject dictionary can be attractively handled. Although subject dictionaries, the most idiosyncratic of all kinds of dictionary whatsoever, vary much in treatment, yet they must be practical and useful. Unfortunately, the nature of the subject precludes quotation.

The limited edition was sold out on publication. In 1955, the publishers and I conferred long and solemnly and finally decided that the book deserved a wider market. For the popular edition, I made a few corrections and additions. There are, admittedly, a few of both still to be made. Meanwhile, the book sells quietly and satisfactorily, all over the world. Not wildly. I succeeded in my attempt to treat the subject as aseptically and remotely (but not inhumanly) as possible.

The next middle-weight I undertook was also a subject dictionary. But how very different from *Shakespeare's Bawdy* was *Name into Word*, published in 1949! Whereas the former was designed as a strictly scholarly and purposive book, the latter, although not unscholarly, was designed to entertain while it informed: and, in this matter, information was very important, nor always quite so easy to come by as I had hoped. If it had all been easily obtained, I should probably have grown weary of it; I enjoyed every minute of this light-hearted enterprise. That's saying something, for it is a long book, as one might expect from its very nature, the sub-title being

Proper Names That Have Become Common Property
A Discursive Dictionary
With a Foreword

The term 'Foreword' – so much disliked by H. W. Fowler – is deliberate, for it combines what is essentially a preface with what is essentially an introduction yet is rather too short to be thus dignified. I wasn't trying to be eccentric; much less, original. It just so happened that the prefatory and the introductory matter fell naturally into a new pattern: in any event, patterns and forms and genres are subservient to matter, not matter to labels: and in its execution, as in its plan, I intended this to be a leisurely, free-and-easy book, agreeable to read and yet factually substantial.

A second edition was required within the year, despite the fact that some of the reviewers objected to the division of the dictionary into two parts: the words (and phrases) widely accepted as having their origins in Proper Names, occupying pages 1–476; and, on pages 479–644, the 'Appendix: Border-Liners and Potential Candidates', consisting both of terms very much less known and of terms not yet held to be acceptable. To any such arrangement, objections can be made; the timid lexicographer avoids the giving of (technical) offence; the bolder asks himself, 'Is there more to be said for than against it?' and, if the answer is a ringing Yes, he carries his plan through to the end. By 1954 the book had gone out of print and, there being by that time no insatiable demand for it, it was allowed to remain there, much to my regret.

Perhaps an example of the leisurely lexicography may be cited:

CARACUL or KARAKUL, usually apprehended in connexion with fur, is – compare *astrakhan* – the product from the wool of the newborn lambs of the *karakul* sheep, a hardy, broad-tailed breed suited to semi-arid regions and, whatever its place of origin, associated with the province of Bokhara. The breed takes its name from a lake in the Pamirs: *Kara Kul*, literally "Black Lake": not far from the city of Bokhara. Weekley cites from Matthew Arnold's *Sohrab and Rustum* (1853) an apposite passage:

'And on his head he plac'd his sheep-skin cap
Black, glossy, curl'd, the fleece of Kara-Kul'.

With the name *Kara Kul*, compare the *Kara Koram* ('black gravel') mountain system and *Karadeniz*, the Turkish name of what we know as 'the *Black* Sea' – for that is what *Karadeniz* literally means, *kara* being Turkish for 'black'. Of all the elements of geographical compound names, *kara* is one of the commonest. That, you will agree, affords a notable addition to your Department of Useless Information; as if there were – as if, indeed, there could be – such a thing as useless information!

VII: PROBLEMS OF ASSEMBLAGE

In MUCH of my work, I have had to go far beyond the written sources and to keep my ears unwaxed, my audile attention alert, and also to get in touch with such persons as can supply material not otherwise obtainable. This was notably true of *Songs and Slang of the British Soldier*, *A Dictionary of Slang*, *Forces' Slang*; and no less true of the second very large work I undertook: *A Dictionary of the Underworld*.

Yet, before I write anything about that mildly spectacular undertaking, I should like to glance at a rather special sort of lexicography, a sort admittedly ancillary and minor: that in which one is invited to bring up to date a dictionary written by someone else; someone either dead or no longer able to attempt the work. I say 'invited to bring up to date', because no lexicographer, however experienced or however fatuous, would, of himself, propose to engage in labour so ungrateful.

In 1951, I was invited to revise and enlarge Hugh Buss's Appendix (1936) to Henry Cecil Wyld's *The Universal Dictionary of the English Language* (1932); this new edition, the third, itself tantamount to a seventh impression, appeared a year later. I found it necessary to excise a few entries: Buss would seem to have been 'bitten by the bug' of Social Credit: he had certainly included too many terms already, by 1951, obsolescent. Apart from that, he had made a good job of the appendix and very little needed to be revised.

Far more important was the question: What new material should be added? And where on earth could I find it?

In a general, all-purposes dictionary that yet leans towards the history of civilization rather than towards that of technology; in such a dictionary as 'the Oxford' in any of its forms, ranging from the massive to the minuscule, and in 'Wyld'; the lexicographer-in-aid must clearly maintain the character of the main work. To do this, he naturally keeps an eye on the New Words sections of all the important dictionaries and has to devise quite different definitions, for the definitions in any dictionary are no less protected by the copyright laws than are the latest effusions of the latest popular poet. More; the very choice, and the arrangement, of words and phrases in a dictionary are themselves copyright. The lexicographer in any well-trodden field must therefore mind his step and tread very warily indeed. (Conversely, in regions either uncharted or badly charted, one has a pretty free hand, as I did in *A Dictionary of Slang* and in *Underworld* and, in a rather different way, in *Origins* and in half-a-dozen other dictionaries I have written.) In addition to those particular New Word sections, there are similar, obviously much more frequent, sections in several of the best-known *Year Books*, notably that of *The Encyclopaedia Britannica*; and very good they are! Then, too, the more enlightened newspapers and magazines have, since the 1890's, paid a prompt and usually well-informed attention to any striking neologism. The word that has, I suppose, received the best press since 1940, is *penicillin*. The entry in the 1952 Appendix to

'Wyld' shows that I wasn't entirely unaware of its lexical importance. Besides those three main sources of new material, a number of important new books were read; they yielded disappointingly few terms not already treated elsewhere. Finally, I addressed pertinent inquiries to several persons likely to know far more than I did about this or that specialist field.

I shall not claim that my Appendix to 'Wyld' scaled the heights. It was, however, a fairly good piece of what might best be described as '*interim* work'. For it I received no adverse, much favourable, comment. But a more thorough and in every other way a better job will have been done in the revision currently progressing at the hands of Ralph W. V. Elliott, the author of that scholarly and most delightful book, *Runes*, and, formerly senior 'language man' at Keele, now the senior lecturer in language at Adelaide.

Two years earlier – that is, early in 1950 – my *Dictionary of the Underworld, British and American* had appeared. More often than about even *A Dictionary of Slang* have I, about *Underworld*, been asked, 'But how did you go about collecting and assembling the material for such a book? The task had never, at least on this scale, been attempted, so how did you attempt it?' Some of the inquirers clearly hoped that I should be able to tell them wonderful stories of a disguised penetration into criminal circles, of long days on the road in the company of tramps, of begging a 'black' in the streets of London and elsewhere, and of scabrous intimacies with drug addicts and white-slavers – and others still less desirable.

Sorry! But I haven't known more than half a dozen crooks in the whole of my life, apart from those whom I

encountered in the aseptic environment of the Army and the
Air Force. As I've already mentioned, I met and, indeed,
knew several crooks while I was serving in the AIF during
the First World War; I've listened to cant being spoken
by groups of crooks and their hangers-on and by groups of
petty and potential crooks: the flashy fellows of the race-
course gangs and the urban gangs, the bludgers and the
lairs, the look-out men (*cockatoos*) and the others. They were
sure that I didn't understand a word they said and it's quite
true that at first I didn't. I did, however, come to assimilate
far more than they suspected.

I was enabled, at no risk whatsoever, to establish contact
with five or six crooks or knowledgeable 'near-crooks' and,
for a beer or two, a half-crown here and there, to obtain
certain information I needed. Yet most of even that information was merely corroborative.

You see, things had been made easy for me by the success
of *A Dictionary of Slang*. I received letters containing direct
information or offers of help should I need it. I always
accepted the offers. A surprisingly large proportion of my
correspondents neither asked nor expected a reward, however small; a few hinted that they would be proud to receive
a copy of some small book written by myself – as, for
instance, *Name This Child*; several more or less literate tramps
admitted that a postal order for half a crown or, in one
instance only, five shillings would be very acceptable.

There have, moreover, been numerous books written by
ex-crooks, by tramps, by police officers and prison officers
(mostly chaplains), and by social workers. For Britain and
the Dominions, I read just about everything that was avail-

able; often I followed up this reading by seeking information either fuller or more precise from those authors – and, of course, from one or two of those few journalists who had written articles on crime. Several letters to the Press, especially in the Dominions, yielded a rich harvest; so rich that usually an unknown term, which rightly I suspected, would be corroborated by more than one informant. There were other sources I tapped, other means I employed; but as I'm not writing a treatise but a sort of critical and selective memoir, I don't propose to exhaust either my subject or my readers.

Yet one other point must be cleared up. 'What about American cant? Did you even go to America?' No; I did not even go to America. 'Then what *did* you do?'

Here, again, I was lucky. Lucky in two ways. Not only could I, as a starting-point, use the wonderful bibliography of slang and cant, *The Literature of Slang*, prepared for the New York Public Library by William Jeremiah Burke ('Jerry' to his familiars); but also I had a very good American friend willing and able to help me to an extent that made of of him my American eyes, almost my 'private eye' – Godfrey Irwin, whose *American Tramp and Underworld Slang*, with a number of tramp songs, I had published in 1931. (I hope that I'm not insufferably egocentric to mention the fact that this is the first book in which my work has been imitated in subject or in method.) The late Godfrey Irwin, a delightful fellow and a real man, had for some years been a tramp, and then for some years a crime reporter, in the United States; he had, moreover, retained many of his old 'contacts'. For me, he read all those books and consulted all those periodicals which were unavailable in Britain. He went further and sought out certain additional sources. He went further still and allowed me to use, as freely as I wished, the typescript of a supplementary collection of material that he never succeeded in getting published, try as both he and I did to obtain a publisher for it.

I also enjoyed the help of a couple of rather good friends, including an ex-crook possessing valuable American and Canadian experience; he lent me a considerable manuscript collection of American and Canadian cant. Wilfred Granville presented me with a paper-covered booklet that, containing a surprising amount of new material, was written by a certain Englishman 'operating' in America; a booklet scarcely known, even to the greatest libraries. Besides all those advantages, I had discovered for myself the most valuable single source for the American underworld of the 1920's and 1930's, precisely as I had discovered the most valuable, by far the most valuable, source for the British underworld of the late seventeenth-early twentieth Centuries.

I wrongly defined or wrongly 'originated' a few 'technical' terms employed by the American drug-addicts and drug-peddlers, partly because that 'world' was unfamiliar to me and partly because I did not wish to overburden Godfrey Irwin. Those errors have been rectified in the second edition. It was inevitable that I should, in America, have aroused hostility in one or two 'authorities' – for reasons now well known to the scholars, and others, whose opinion matters. In the main, however, I received congratulatory letters from crime reporters and other journalists and also from half a dozen or more ex-crooks; at least, they claimed to be 'ex-'.

Apart from its linguistic interest, *Underworld* has a value not even yet fully realized. It supplies a vast amount of social and sociological information upon, and a large number of potential sources for, a history of crime – and a history of the outcasts – of the United States during the period 1790 onwards. Much of the material is horrifying; much of it, disgusting; some of it, picturesque, but most of it sordid; a small part of it, little better than ephemeral, but most of it (95 %, at the very least) astonishingly long-lived. One could, I suppose, fairly say that *Underworld* is an exciting work – but not to be read by the sensitive.

VIII: ETYMOLOGICAL—A
MATTER OF ORIGINS

✳✳✳✳✳✳✳✳✳✳✳✳✳✳✳✳✳✳✳✳✳✳✳✳✳✳✳✳✳✳✳✳✳✳✳✳✳

BY THE Reverend A. Smythe Palmer* in *Folk-Etymology*,
1882, it was shrewdly remarked that 'Man is an etymo-
logizing animal', a statement falling into the thought-pattern
of – and at least as true as – Aristotle's 'Man is by nature a
political animal' and probably truer than Seneca's 'Man is a
reasoning animal'. The statement is far less paradoxical than
it might at first seem to be, for the tendency to *etymologize*,
to discover the origins of words and phrases and sayings,
forms merely one aspect and one branch, little-regarded yet
valid, of that curiosity with which, luckily for ourselves, we
are all of us born; if, that is, we are born with a mind at all.
In many of the annals and chronicles of primeval history we
find evidence of an embryonic etymology; nor quite always
is it folk-etymology.

That I should early have acquired a taste for the origins
and histories of words and phrases was probably inevitable,
for even as a young child I possessed an uncomfortably
inquisitive mind. That it should have taken me some thirty
years to transcend the stage of the purest amateurism was

* In my *Adventuring Among Words*, 1961, I have done something
towards a just estimate of this very considerable, and considerably forgotten, scholar.

85

perhaps equally inevitable, for both education and a strong inclination long kept me on a literary rather than a linguistic course. I have not abandoned literature; nor shall I do so, for I am, after all, one of those who think that the divorce between language and literature should never have taken place. (That scholars normally specialize in one rather than in the other is natural enough, the subjects being vast and complex. Knowledge demands eternity, but human life is dauntingly brief.)

I was fortunate in that I began my university course as an honours student in Classics; that I had become interested in French at a reasonably early stage; that during my first undergraduate year I took up German because, although not requiring the subject academically, I felt that I did require it personally; that during the First World War I allowed nothing to prevent me from at least maintaining those four languages and that, for intellectual exercise and aesthetic pleasure, I learned to read Italian and Spanish with a very fair fluency; that I kept my mind supple with a small amount (largely cogitated) of philosophy – for instance, Bertrand Russell's *The Problems of Philosophy* and, in French, Spinoza's *Ethics*, a metaphysical system demonstrated 'geometrically' but based on ethics. To Spinoza's brilliant and closely argued work, *The Problems of Philosophy* served as an easy introduction. One can really get one's teeth into something when one tackles Spinoza's *Ethics*: and how immensely one benefits from grappling with this ice-cold yet strangely eloquent masterpiece! Much later, I came to read and enjoy such philosophers as Alfred North Whitehead and Robin George Collingwood. Indeed I have, for years,

thought of writing a long critical essay on, perhaps even a
short study of, Collingwood's books, ranging from the
historical to the autobiographical, but concentrating upon
the philosophical works, from the literary and linguistic,
much rather than from the professional, angle.

Those war years represent a period of germination. I did
not form a passion for etymology and related subjects until
(as I have already mentioned) I collaborated with John
Brophy in *Songs and Slang of the British Soldier*. During the
next twenty years, I expressed that passion in several works,
yet only cursorily and briefly and secondarily. It reveals
itself here and there in *A Dictionary of Slang* – in *Name into
Word* – in *Underworld*.

Once *Underworld* had finally gone to press, I pondered the
idea of an etymological dictionary of modern English and
soon I planned it in detail and, to encourage myself, decided
upon the title *Origins*. This is my best-planned work. It is in
such planning, at once careful and imaginative, that one
perceives how much one has benefited by learning to
organize one's mind and therefore be able to control a large
and complex undertaking: and such organizing ability as I
possess derives almost equally from two kinds of training:
the general mental discipline inculcated by a serious (although
necessarily sporadic) study of philosophy, especially that of
metaphysics; and the particular lexicographical training I
had given myself by working on the various dictionaries
already mentioned.

If he works without benefit of scriptorium, without the
emulation and encouragements of collaborators, without
even the lessening, by assistants, of that drudgery which

renders all long-term lexicography a labour exacting patience and fortitude, a lexicographer needs to possess more than those two trainings: he needs both sympathy and vision, the former to empower him to understand the difficulties experienced by his consulters and readers, the latter to show him how best he can overcome those difficulties without impairing the systematic yet imaginative presentation of his material; material that is inevitably intractable, for it mirrors and expresses the thoughts and desires and achievements of mankind. 'There is a hell of a lot of human nature in men, women and children' – and much of it unpredictable, some of it unfathomable, most of it sturdily resistant to regimentation and standardization.

Still more than in the dictionaries of *Slang* and *Underworld*, I profited by the initial period which I had spent in planning how to arrange and display the matter I intended to present and how, of course, to perform the task both intelligently and attractively. I wished the final result of my plans and my labours to be both convincing to the mind of the scholar and agreeable to the aesthetic and literary tastes of the general public; and, I should not have to add, *vice versa*. I also wished to pack as much as possible into a space that rendered the undertaking commercially possible: not too ruinously costly to the publishers nor too exorbitantly expensive for the book-buying public. In justice to my publishers, I hasten to add that they very generously gave me an astonishingly free hand. But then, I have been lucky in my publishers. (What they themselves think is quite another matter, nor should I be so impertinent or so fatuous as to pretend to think for them.)

Etymology in general has, by *The Shorter Oxford English Dictionary*, been defined as 'the process of expounding the elements of a word with their modifications of form and sense', a sufficient definition, providing that 'expounding' be taken to include 'determining the earliest form of those elements'; and etymology in particular has, by *Webster's New International* (second edition), been defined as 'the history of a word, showing its source and its development in form and meaning'. As a definition of the narrower sense of *etymology*, the latter supplies a first-rate practical guide for our purpose, for I do not propose to discuss the art and science, the theory and the practice, of etymology. For general principles, as for the problems, of etymology, I refer the earnest inquirer to such works as W. W. Skeat's *Primer of Classical and English Etymology*, which, published early in the century, remains trustworthy, although perhaps a trifle over-simplified; to John W. Clark's remarkable summary in *The Encyclopedia Americana*; to the relevant passages in J. R. Hulbert's delightful *Dictionaries, British and American;* and, at a more advanced level, Alan S. C. Ross's *Etymology, with especial reference to English*. For those general readers and students who, not instead of but in addition to one or more of those works, might care to associate themselves with what could justly be called 'the human aspects of etymology', I venture to recommend, especially as a tailpiece to my etymological dictionary, a little book that bears a human title: *Adventuring among Words*; the more so as, contrary to expectations (including mine), it has met with a genial response and has infiltrated into circles where, a generation earlier, it would have encountered nothing warmer than an icy stare or a chilly 'Well, what would you expect of a mere amateur?'

It was, I need hardly emphasize, slightly intrusive and obtrusive of me to undertake *Origins* while Skeat's *Etymological Dictionary of the English Language* remained in print; it had been mildly audacious of Ernest Weekley to publish his, early in the 1920's, and then to challenge Skeat's *Concise Etymological* with his own *Concise*. Whereas Ernest Weekley's large work has gone irretrievably out of print, his smaller one, in its 1952 revision, is the better small work of the two, and not only because it is forty-two years nearer to being up-to-date. Yet Weekley's *Concise* itself needs re-editing, for he did not live to make those further revisions and those additions which he so much wanted to make. I should, before now, have offered myself for the task, were it not for the fact that I might come to prefer to write a 'Concise' of my own. As it is, I am proud to have been able to arrange for the publication of Weekley's improved 'Concise'; he was so grateful that he made me feel ashamed, so little had I, after all, done for him.

Despite the very merits of the large works by Skeat and Weekley, I felt – indeed, I knew – that there was room for an etymological dictionary that, of comparable size, was not merely up-to-date (a very secondary consideration in an etymologicon) in the matter of the terms included, but also arranged in a totally different manner, on the basis not of single words but of groups of words related one to another – a principle that Skeat had promised to pursue, yet, with very few exceptions, failed to observe. This plan, so far from having been suggested by Skeat's major work, was devised

by myself as much the best way of dealing with a problem
that had been steadily ignored: a plan that makes things so
much more agreeable and, for some, more exciting to the
user of an etymological dictionary than a vast mass of, in the
main, lonely entities. Both *The Oxford English Dictionary*
and *Webster's New International* occasionally refer the
consulter to another word and, although rarely, indicate a
nexus; *Webster* the more frequently and consistently of the
two. When they do this, they do it – I need hardly say –
extremely well.

But nobody purchases either of those works, the one
enormous and the other massive, simply for the etymologies
they contain. Again I need hardly say that, for individual
etymologies, both of those great achievements are admirable:
and when a user is dissatisfied with the entry in *Origins*, he
should hasten to rebut me with the aid of O.E.D. or *Webster*;
I should take that dissatisfaction as a compliment, for, better
than most, I know how far from certainty falls many an
apparent certitude. Nobody, however, consults a general
dictionary for etymologies when all he wants is an etymology: he goes to an etymologicon, for there he will find
precisely what he seeks: and he finds it in the most instructive
and readable form, the entries being, as it were, geared to his
requirements and perhaps to his desires. Yet an etymological
dictionary conveys, too, a modicum of commentary or
explanation – just sufficient to put the word 'on the map'. If
the problem is semantic, all the necessary information about
meanings and sub-meanings (or, if you prefer, about senses
and nuances) is set forth as clearly and as compactly as possible.

Although the majority of English words belong to a

group, however small, yet, as in every language, a certain number are singletons. Whereas *certain* obviously has many relations, *okapi* has none. (In etymology, as elsewhere, such absolute statements carry within themselves an implicit modification, whether the modification be, in the fact, required or not. For instance, *okapi* is probably related to other African words; it is not, so far as I know, related to any other word forming an integral part of the English language.) Such singletons are treated much the same in all etymological dictionaries; but the treatment of *certain* will differ according to the general plan and to the principles upon which the plan itself is based. Most of the exotics – words adopted from some 'native' language – are singletons. They may be and often are quite fascinating in themselves, for they are often connected with adventure and exploration, with settlement and commerce; but they lack that wider and deeper interest which attaches to words forming part of a civilized group or, especially, of a constellation.

Had Ernest Weekley's larger book remained in print, I might never have formed the intention, which I did form so early as the late 1930's, of writing an etymological dictionary, for he adopted much the same sort of manner as I was to adopt. As Weekley carried Skeat's method and matter a stage further, so I went rather beyond Weekley; in grouping, very much further. I can now, without offence or indiscretion, reveal that I tried to get Weekley's larger book either reprinted, with addenda, or republished, with corrections and additions incorporated into the text. Improbable though it may seem, I had no luck at all. (His smaller book did not present the same difficulties.)

I also learned that Skeat's large etymological dictionary was not to be revised, but that Dr Onions was preparing one to take its place. That was away back in 1938. Repeated inquiries brought the information that Dr Onions's work was not yet ready – that no one knew when it would be ready – that doubts were held as to its ever being ready. Naturally I checked with Dr Onions himself, for I certainly did not intend to even try to compete with a work written by him. He was very good about the matter and finally he told me that he didn't know and couldn't tell when he would complete his task. He added that probably he never would complete it and most generously enjoined me to feel free to begin a work that, as he had long realized, I was postponing out of deference to him.

So, at last, I began a task that I knew would be long, complex, arduous; a work that, along general lines, I had been planning for many years; an achievement very dear to me. I spent at least a month in determining exactly how I should go about it; the problems of scope and style had already been solved by a prolonged process of meditation, of proposal and rejection, of doubt and clarification. That done, I set myself to devise an adequate set of abbreviations and references: one that would save a great deal of space, yet, at the same time, enable the user of the dictionary – once he had assimilated the 'shorthand' – to read fluently what I fully intended he should be able to read fluently.

Perhaps I should interpolate the fact that, before I meditated, I had assembled the material; in other words, formed the vocabulary of words to be treated – in, of course, alphabetical order. That skeleton vocabulary was richly annotated with cross-references, with suggestions about dependence and interdependence, with possible additions, and so forth. That sort of preliminary list is necessary. It also saves a tremendous amount of time and spares one from a multiple frustration. It can so easily be enlarged or reduced.

By the way, I never use a card-index, a device idolized by those students whose sole merit is method. It is physically clumsy and mentally a constant source of bafflement. That it best serves the needs of a team engaged in a vast project, I readily admit. Only, I'm not a team. I do my own work. No; I use large exercise books, with sufficient spacing between entries, and the left-hand page a blank. If one's planning has been both careful and comprehensive, one has ample room left for additions and modifications: and one can see a considerable area of work displayed: the trees do not obscure the view of the wood. Cards serve well enough for singletons. For long complex entries, they are inferior, and for large groups, still more for vast constellations, they are hopeless. Quite apart from all that, one can, in the physical sense, work very much more rapidly with such exercise-books than with such cards, for the books are so much easier to write in and one can turn forward or back so much more easily and speedily. Books have many other points of superiority over cards, but, as I'm not writing a student's manual on the subject, I'll leave the matter at that; and anyway I'm not trying to make converts. Why, indeed, should I, even as an exercise in altruism? Most such projects as *A Dictionary of Slang, Underworld, Origins,* are now undertaken by teams. Few scholars nowadays seem to have the physical endurance, the moral courage, the spiritual stamina, of such men as Skeat and Weekley. Clearly, I'm not talking about such huge enterprises as *The O.E.D.* or *Webster's*, which simply have to be prosecuted by a team. Nor yet about such a work as Joseph Wright's *English Dialect Dictionary*, for that great and extraordinarily industrious scholar (who, although truly dedicated, remained a lively and lovable person) possessed two advantages: the resources of the English Dialect Society and the constant and invaluable collaboration of his learned and devoted wife.

Where one man can do a job alone, and where he is capable of doing a good job, the result must, in some respects, be superior to that produced by a team, but in others probably – not certainly – inferior to the collective product. A team should be able to ensure a greater degree of comprehensiveness and a higher degree of accuracy, especially by checking sources and in correcting proofs. A team can, if it works methodically and diligently, cover a much wider field of research – if a very wide field *has* to be covered. On the other hand, no team is stronger than its weakest link; if there are several weak links, an almost intolerable strain is imposed on the general editor. Every team is ultimately dependent on its general editor, whether he is working autonomously and, in the best sense, authoritatively, or whether he is, in effect, an executive (rather than a general) editor enforcing the recommendations of an advisory committee. I simply couldn't work as the member of a team: I prefer to make my own mistakes. Nor do I very much care for the exasperations and exacerbations, the delays and the disappointments, inseparable from working with any group.

But although a collective work should, theoretically, be

more accurate and comprehensive than a one-man job, there are certain tasks that, even on those grounds, are done better by the lone worker: where, for instance, it is extremely difficult, if not impossible, to assemble a team with the necessary knowledge and the advisable flair. Many very able persons would not recognize the evidence when they saw it, nor, therefore, be able to differentiate a certain class of matter from a closely related yet essentially different class. Perhaps those are aspects too arcane for discussion in such a book as this, but they are present in, they form an inherent part of, every such dictionary as *Slang* and *Underworld*.

Yet one can at least mention lexicographical points at which the 'lone wolf' must, if he knows his business, write a better book, provided that it remain within his physical abilities. He adopts an attitude, and makes an approach, that only he can single-mindedly maintain and undeviatingly prosecute; the style is, throughout, that of one man, not of several or many; the manner and the tone are personal – they may be idiosyncratic – they need be neither eccentric nor uncontrolled. In short, he can and, if he is writer as well as scholar, will strongly impress upon his work a definite character and a clear-cut personality. True; that personality will offend the worshippers of uniformity: those self-deluders who think that, by being dull and drab, they are proving themselves dispassionate, judicious, well-balanced. Poise and equity and, so far as we human beings can attain it, dispassion are hard-won qualities flowing from mind and spirit, not badges assumed at will nor mere features of style nor the privileges of intellectual mediocrity. It is, I think, better for people to be irritated into disagreement and prodded into thought than for them to be bored into un-protesting acceptance and drugged into mental sleep and spiritual apathy. Exacerbation is, I feel, preferable to accidia. There is no death more horrible than the death of the spirit.

But the preceding paragraph does not imply a rejection of the humane disciplines of genuine scholarship. Only within some kind of law can one be truly free. I like to think that in *Origins* I have chosen a plan and adopted a technique that exhibit imagination and perhaps vision; no less firmly do I hope that those qualities have been harnessed in the services of scholarship and, in the fact, induced to subserve that very special sort of scholarship which lexi-cography demands and etymology requires.

The grouping of related words will be found to vary tremendously. In its simplest form it may be exemplified by *blast*. Whereas Weekley relates it only to *blaze*, I relate it to *blaze, blow, blush, bluster*, yet I treat the five words separately. But whereas Weekley deals with *dynamic, dynamite, dynamo, dynasty*, as separate entries, I deal with those four, add *dyne*, and assemble them into one forceful group.

Those are comparatively simple groupings. The next stage appears in such an arrangement as that of *cordial* and its cognates, which are in Weekley represented by an equal number of entries and are only partly grouped in *Origins*, where the *cordial* entry includes *misericord, courage* (and its derivatives), *cardiac*, but allows separate entries for *accord, concord, discord, record*, and refers the reader to the less closely related *heart*.

But why such inconsistency? Well, I happen to be one of those scholars who think that the reader's convenience should override the lexicographer's virtuosity. Admittedly this consideration for others seems to have been forgotten when we come to the constellation I've permitted myself at *rex*. Where Weekley has separate entries at *rajah*, *real* (the coin), *realm*, *rectangle*, *recto*, *rector*, *rectum*, *regal*, *regalia*, *regent*, *régime*, *regiment*, *region*, *regius*, *regnant*, *regular*, *regulus*, *reich*, *reign*, *right*, *royal*, *rule*, etc., I deploy them around the central *rex* and the basic *regere*, to guide, and thus show the relationship to such further words as *correct*, *direct*, *erect* – to *dirge* and *adroit* – to *dress* and *redress*. But I do show some pity, for I refer the reader to the separate entries *rich* and *reach* and *surge*.

Grouping is perhaps seen at its best when the group contains either clusters of words from Greek, from Latin, from the Germanic languages, and perhaps from Sanskrit, or some modification or variation of those clusters, for here the inquirer is faced with words of forms so different, one from another, that he may not have realized that a connexion even exists. Without going into tedious detail, I suggest that *Origins* be consulted at such entries as *via*, *vibrate*, *vide*, *vigor*, *vine*, *viva*, *vocable*, *voluble*.

Both Skeat and Weekley were first-rate scholars, the former being a shade the more erudite, the latter much the more alert. Both of them, in their etymological dictionaries, aimed to be readable – and were. In these matters, I could be said to have imitated them, although I did not, in fact, imitate them. Only in the admittedly important matter of all words other than singletons do I differ from them. Let me show what I mean by quoting a very carefully chosen entry from Weekley's large work and then the corresponding entry from my own: the adjective *rum*. I write all words in full, to spare my readers the fatigue of guessing precisely what this or that abbreviation abbreviates.

'RUM. Adjective. Apparently special use of obsolete *rum*, good, a very common cant word (16th century) which was prefixed, with varying sense, to a great number of nouns and is supposed to be identical with *rom* [male gipsy. Romany *rom*, man]. *The Dictionary of the Canting Crew* gives fifty-two such compounds, including *rum cove*, which originally meant a great rogue.'

In *Origins* the word figures thus:

'RUM, adjective. See ROME, paragraph 10.' That paragraph reads: 'The colloquial-from-slang-from-cant *rum*, inferior, odd, shady, originally denoted "superior, excellent, (very) fine"; the 16th–18th Century variant *rome* (compare the 17th Century *room* or *roome*) suggests that, as John Camden Hotten proposed, *rum*, excellent, fine, derives either from *Rome* or from Latin-Medieval Latin *rom*anus. For the form *rum*, compare Turkish *rumi*, belonging to the ancient Romans, and Arabic *Rumi*, belonging to Rome; for the sense, note Poe's "the grandeur that was Rome" and the many favourable connotations of *Roman* and of such phrases as *Romano more*, in the Roman way, that is candidly, frankly.'

My etymology is too summarily exhibited, for it does not explain *why* the sense '(very) good' should become '(very) bad'. I repaired that defect when, in 1961, I published *Adventuring among Words:*

'The explanation is simple. *Rum* originated in the underworld: any thing or person approved and esteemed by the underworld was, to and for them, good, very good, the best: but all such things, actions, persons were naturally held by ordinary, honest, respectable people to be bad, if only because injurious or dangerous to themselves. Thus we are confronted with the apparent contradiction that the favourable adjective *rum* became, in the nineteenth century, virtually synonymous with the unfavourable adjective *queer*, which originally, among criminals and beggars and their dubious periphery, signified the exact opposite, and formed the required complement, of *rum*.'

Skeat's etymology agrees in the main with Weekley's. The plain truth is that neither Skeat nor Weekley nor I know what the origin of *rum* is: but we have all guessed at an etymology and apparently believe in our guesses, not merely believe them. Some day, I shall (D.V.) 'have a crack' at solving the adjectival *rum* – and a few others from among the too numerous terms that so far have baffled the word detectives.

* * *

I suspect that someone is, very properly, going to ask this pertinent question: Apart from the grouping of words, has *Origins* any other features in which it differs from Skeat and Weekley? Whereas Weekley provides no matter additional to a preface, Skeat provides a list of prefixes and a note on suffixes; a list of homonyms, and another of doublets; a compact list of Indo-Germanic (or, as I prefer to call them, Indo-European) roots; and a most informative section entitled 'Distribution of Words'. Not being entirely stupid, I carefully considered homonyms, doublets, distribution, but rejected them as belonging rather to a history of the

English language than to a dictionary; retained prefixes, noted additional examples, and treated the subject in greater detail; supplied a tolerably comprehensive list of suffixes and, as for the prefixes, mentioned their etymologies; and formed a much more extensive list of roots, which I handled both as Indo-European roots and as English word-forming elements and thus rendered (I hope) a more practical service to students, the mere roots being all very well for trained philologists but rather less useful to students and to the intelligent section of the general reading public, for whom, as a friendly scholar has remarked, I have shown how they can solve for themselves the etymologies of many thousands of words not even mentioned in *Origins*: a sort of 'do-it-yourself kit'. What's more, the kit really works, as many delighted customers have told me in unsolicited testimonials.

IX: PROBLEMS OF AGE; OR, DICTIONARIES FOR CHILDREN
(A Marginal Note)

THE YOUNGER the child, the harder it is to write for it. That dictum, the truth of which is usually learnt at the cost of much experiment and many disappointments, applies no less to dictionaries than to ordinary books of fiction or poetry, of history or biology, of travel or animal life. Indeed, it is far more difficult to write such a dictionary for children as is both readable and accurate than to write a true or an imaginary story or a tolerably accurate description of creatures or scenes in which a child naturally tends to be interested. The subject-matter of the ordinary book for children is presumably suitable to children: its author starts at a tremendous advantage over that unfortunate person who has to overcome a natural disinclination or, worse, a natural resistance to the acquisition of a knowledge regarded as merely useful or, at best, very far from exciting or enchanting, from compelling or fascinating.

It would not be very difficult to write, for children, a dictionary designed to engage their attention. What is difficult is to supply definitions so accurate, yet so simple, so easy to learn or to assimilate, that one does not bend or twist or dent the truth.

A very elementary dictionary – a 'youngest' dictionary – should include a number of clear, uncomplicated line-drawings and, for those words (for instance, the names of flowers or of precious and semi-precious stones) which involve the idea of colour, a few coloured plates. To the young child, untrained in the forming and analysing of ideas, this sort of visual aid is essential; yet he too is well advised to learn the definitions, for often no form of visual aid is possible.

As I write this little book, I have not yet had the salutary experience of attempting a dictionary for very young children (of, say, six-nine years of age), but I have spent some considerable time on a dictionary for children of the age-group that ranges from a very intelligent ten, or an averagely intelligent eleven, years, to a fairly intelligent thirteen. At the same time, I was aiming at those other pupils or students who, no matter what their age, do not speak English as their native language: for whom it is better to be just a shade too elementary than a shade too advanced. To make things still more difficult for myself by rendering the book adequate to the needs of children all over the world, I did my best to avoid the attitude of a 'Little Englander' – or, come to that, of any intensely nationalist, hence inevitably parochial, American or Australian, New Zealander or South African or Canadian, or any European or Asiatic or African or South American or what-have-you. To do all this, on the level of that age-group or knowledge-group, is in one sense impossible but, in another, well worth the endeavour.

Any dictionary for children poses certain special problems absent from a dictionary for adults. I shall not enumerate all of those problems. Here are a few of the greater, the more important, the more searching.

One must, in the definitions, employ no word that is not explained elsewhere in the dictionary. This precaution applies, of course, to any selective one-language dictionary; but to children's dictionaries it applies still more forcefully than to adults' dictionaries.

More important, ultimately, is the difficulty of defining words embodying a philosophical concept – as, especially, do all conjunctions and prepositions. Such words present a tremendous problem even in dictionaries for adults: to define them for children is impossible, no matter how hard one tries: the most one can do is to explain by indirection; that is, not so much explain, in the usual sense of that verb, as convey by examples, so that the child gradually assimilates the sense by forming, unconsciously, his own conclusions and by finally getting the slippery fish of sense into the semantic net and recognizing it and transfixing it. Almost any example tends, when taken by itself, to appear inadequate. Perhaps *by* will serve as well as almost any other.

BY (1), preposition. Near or next to, as 'an inn *by* the road'; alongside, as 'a road *by* the lake'; in or at, as '*by* day and *by* night'; from, as 'Detected *by* his mannerisms'; at or a little before, as 'You must leave *by* midnight'; because of, or through the action or agency of, as 'He won *by* sheer courage' – 'a novel *by* Fielding' – 'receive a packet *by* messenger'; according to, as 'Don't judge a book *by* its cover'; at an amount, or in a measure, of, as 'He sold grapes *by* the pound and apples *by* the dozen'. Hence:

BY (2), adverb. Near, as 'Stand *by*, men!'; aside, apart, as

'Put all your troubles *by*'; beyond, past, as 'He sauntered *by*' and 'How time goes *by*!'

Only the simplest, clearest language should be used. But it must be simple, not silly; nor yet childish. No child enjoys being either spoken or written to as though it lacked intelligence. Most children are, in the main, quite startlingly intelligent until their minds become stunted or inhibited by their less lively and imaginative seniors. Moreover, any adult permitting himself a condescending smile or careless pat on the head to the child he is addressing, whether in speech or on the printed page, thereby convicts himself of stupidity and insensitiveness and proves that, although he may conceivably possess a grain of common sense, he certainly possesses no good sense whatsoever.

The first thing a writer (or, come to that, an editor) for children should bear in mind is that the children are his allies: they have, in the best sense of the adjective, immensely inquisitive minds: they hunger for knowledge and are prepared to go to quite a lot of trouble to get it: and, during the course of acquisition, they do not wish to be 'talked down to': indeed, they appreciate and respond to the from-one-equal-to-another approach, for it connotes both a compliment and a challenge.

Allied to that psychological fact is the necessity to avoid being facetious. The adult's sense of humour differs enormously from the child's; and extremely few adults can bridge the gulf. 'Play it safe!'

X: REVISION; OR, THE PENALTIES OF NON-FAILURE

✺✺✺✺✺✺✺✺✺✺✺✺✺✺✺✺✺✺✺✺✺✺✺✺✺✺✺✺✺✺✺✺✺

'It is not my first, but my second, editions which are rare.'
ALEXANDER WOOLLCOTT.

MORE THAN almost any other kind of book, a dictionary constantly needs to be revised; especially, of course, if it deals with the current form of a language and therefore has to be kept up to date.

The amount, like the frequency, of revision varies greatly from work to work. Since this is not a do-it-yourself guide to lexicography nor even a comprehensive survey of such revisions as I have undertaken, I shall confine my brief remarks to four representative books, treated in their chronological order: *A Dictionary of Slang and Unconventional English – Usage and Abusage – A Dictionary of the Underworld, British and American* – and *Origins: A Short Etymological Dictionary of Modern English*.

All except the first of these revisions could (theoretically, at least) have been made by myself working alone; in *Origins*, however, I have owed almost more to my friends and other correspondents than to myself. But *A Dictionary of Slang* could not possibly have been revised at all adequately without the assistance of correspondents from all over the

English-speaking world. I did, of course, go to some considerable trouble, both in gathering new material and in correcting or otherwise improving the existing entries by addition and modification, by noting earlier or later dates, by amplifying and by narrowing, and so forth. (This sort of thing so easily becomes a catalogue!) For instance, I read a vast number of books and articles with certain specific ends in view.

All the material coming from friends and acquaintances and other well-wishers (and from a few less eager to help me than to display their own superior knowledge) had to be checked and sifted, collated and refined, and, most of it, re-written. A rudimentary example of correction and addition is afforded by

'*Jimmy the One*. The First Lieutenant: naval: c.20. Bowen. Cf. *one-pipper*.' Here, 'c.20' stands for 20th Century; and 'Bowen' for Frank Bowen, *Sea Slang*, 1929. The Supplement contains the following entry:—

Jimmy the One. An earlier reference occurs in 'Taffrail': 'The first lieutenant (a lieutenant commander as he usually is in these days [1916]) is "Jimmy the One".' Often simply *Jimmy* (Granville). Here the reference is to:—

Wilfred Granville's typescript of *A Dictionary of Naval Slang*, made available to me by its generous author and published in an amplified form in 1948 – a work that went out of print in 1951 and was rendered obsolete by his later and better *Dictionary of Sailors' Slang* (1962).

Certain entries can hardly be augmented; only elaborated. But it is usually preferable to leave the original untouched: the mood and the stylistic tempo of long ago can hardly be recaptured. I could, for instance, have added to the list of differentiated sexual characteristics in the following entry, but I should have been foolish to do so:—

cunny-thumbed. Given to closing his fist, as a woman does, with the thumb turned inwards under the first three fingers: low colloquial: late 18th–20th Centuries. Grose, 1st ed. Ex *cunny* [the female genitals]. – 2. 19th–20th Century schoolboys': given to shooting a marble as a girl does.

Other sex tests are these: an object thrown at a woman's shins or knees causes her to close her knees; at her genitals, to open her legs, whereas a man closes his; at her chest, to protect her breasts. A man walks from the hips; a woman (unless an impenitent hiker or an athletic champion) usually from the knees. In threading a needle, a man holds the needle stationary and advances the thread towards the eyelet, whereas a woman directs the needle on to the stationary thread – a difference that has originated a psychologico-physiological riddle. Apart from her voice, hair and breasts, a woman masquerading as a man is apt to forget that the proportionate breadth of shoulders and especially the hips, as well as the contour of the legs from hip to knee, are different in a man. In short, she would do well to wear long full trousers, for, in addition, her knees are much less bony, much more rounded, than a man's.

The revision of *Usage and Abusage: A Guide to Good English* proved to be very much simpler. I had merely to fill certain painfully obvious gaps; bring the book up to date; correct misprints; and remove much pointless bibliographical information. *The Concise Usage and Abusage* has been based upon the drastically revised fifth edition of the original work.

Revision; or, the Penalties of Non-Failure

A Dictionary of the Underworld, British and American presented the same kind of problems as *Slang* had presented. But I had to rest content with bringing only the British section (Britain, Canada, Australia, New Zealand, South Africa) up to date and, of course, revising the original. For American cant, I could revise the work only up to the date already attained: 1950. All the same, *Underworld* does, for the period from the 1530's until 1950, record nearly all the relevant words and phrases of the British and (since the 18th Century) American underworld. It has, therefore, rendered available to historians, sociologists, economists – and to writers scrupulous about 'the right word for the right period' – a vast body of evidence unavailable elsewhere.

Origins: A Short Etymological Dictionary of Modern English appeared very near the end of October, 1958. The second edition, appearing in the middle of the following year, owed much to Professors John W. Clark and Simeon Potter and several other generous friends. The third, which came out in December 1961, was again indebted to the same friends. It also owed something to Professor Norman Davis, of the University of Oxford, to Professor Mario Pei, of Columbia University, New York, and to Mr Stephen Potter, the witty and ingenious author of such masterpieces of 'spoof' and 'leg-pull' as *Gamesmanship, Lifemanship, One-upmanship, Super-manship*; but, most of all, to that sound and selfless scholar, Professor Richard Middleton Wilson, of the University of Sheffield. Indirect assistance, monitory and suggestive, came from the editor of the vast new Supplement, now in preparation, to *The Oxford English Dictionary*: Mr R. W.

Burchfield, who, like Professor Norman Davis and myself, is a New Zealander.

There must, in our small country, be something that leads its native-born males into the fields of language, for, besides the three persons mentioned, one has only to recall the names of Kenneth Sisam, that notable Middle English scholar who was, for a long time, the Secretary of the Clarendon Press; Professor Fraser Mackenzie, head of the French department in the University of Birmingham, and author of the magistral *Les Relations de l'Angleterre et de la France d'après le vocabulaire*, published in two volumes in 1939; and Dr J. A. W. Bennett, Fellow of Magdalen College, Oxford, and lecturer in English.

Perhaps this affinity between New Zealanders and language derives in part from the fact that, of all the British Dominions, New Zealand the most closely resembles Britain in climate and race and character. Its native sons revere the Old Country and its language: and, living on the antipodal periphery, they bring fresh and dispassionate minds both to the study of English Old and Middle and Modern and to the consideration of language in general and in the mass.

XI: THE ART OF LEXICOGRAPHY; A FEW RANDOM BIBLIOGRAPHICAL COMMENTS

❋✼

OF ENCYCLOPAEDIC articles upon the history of lexicography, the following merit a special note; all bear the title Dictionary or Dictionaries:

Dr C. T. Onions in *Chambers's*: brief, lucid, authoritative.

Alexander McQueen in *The Britannica*: much longer and very informative. Here is a name that should be far better known. Alexander McQueen, learned and urbane, is an English migrant, many, many years ago, to the United States, of which he has long been a citizen.

Clarence L. Barnhart, brilliant planner and editor of dictionaries: in *The Americana*.

The best encyclopaedic article not written in English is Bruno Migliorini's masterly sketch ('Lessicografia') in the *Enciclopedia Italiana*.

Perhaps comparable with those articles is an essay ('Dictionaries') in my book, *A Charm of Words*, 1960.

Two notable historical works upon the history of British and American lexicography are Mitford M. Mathews's *Survey of English Dictionaries*, 1923, and *The English*

Dictionary from Cawdrey to Johnson, by De Witt Starnes and G. E. Noyes, 1946.

Dr J. A. Sheard is, for The Language Library, preparing *The Growth of the English Dictionary*.

Combining both a summary history and a short but very able discussion of the problems of lexicography, is Professor J. R. Hulbert's *Dictionaries: British and American*, one of my own favourite books – comprehensive and clear, magistral yet simple, and written with modesty and charm.

The late R. W. Chapman's *Lexicography*, 1948, is shrewd, slight, entertaining. Much more imposing is *Introducción a la Lexicografía Moderna*, published, 1950, in Madrid and written by that very distinguished scholar, Señor Julio Casares.

Shorter, and geared to the needs of Hungarian lexicography, yet invaluable to all students of the subject, is Ladislas Országh's long article published, in English, in a Hungarian review.

There have been several brief personal records of lexicography, such as Johnson's famous Preface. But the only full account written by a famous lexicographer is Emile Littré's *Comment j'ai fait mon Dictionnaire*, a fascinating account that first appeared, in a not very well-known collection, *Etudes et Glanures*, 1880, and was edited, with a generous foreword, by Michel Bréal in 1897.

INDEX

Index

Index

Skeat, W. W., 89, 90, 92–93, 98, 100

slang, 27–28, 67–69

Slang and Unconventional English, A Dictionary of, 37, 38–39, 57–58, 72, 78, 81, 87, 100, 108, 117, 119

Slang Today and Yesterday, 35–37

Smith, David Nichol, 24–25

'Something before nothing', 40–59 *passim*

Songs and Slang of the British Soldier (1914–1918), 27–29, 78, 117

Spinoza, 86

Starnes, De Witt, and G. E. Noyes, 112

subject dictionaries, 74

TEAMS OF SCHOLARS, 95–96

Underworld, A Dictionary of the, 78, 80–84, 87, 109, 118

underworld, language of the, *see* cant

usage, 20

Usage and Abusage, 70–72, 108, 118

Usage and Abusage, The Concise, 72–73, 108, 119

WAVELL, FIELD-MARSHAL LORD, 28–29

Webster, Noah, 20

Webster's New International Dictionary, 10, 37, 42, 49–54, 89, 91, 95

Weekley, Ernest, 11, 29–31, 91, 92, 97–100

Whitehead, A. N., 86

Wilson, Edmund, 15

Wilson, Richard Middleton, 109

World War, the First, 21–23, 86–87

World War, the Second, 64–69

Wright, Joseph, 34, 95

Wyld, H. C. K., 24–25, 74, 78–80

A LIST OF DICTIONARIES
by ERIC PARTRIDGE

✼✼✼✼✼✼✼✼✼✼✼✼✼✼✼✼✼✼✼✼✼✼✼✼✼✼✼✼✼✼✼✼✼✼✼✼✼

Songs and Slang of the British Soldier (1914–1918): with John Brophy. 1930 – 3rd edition, 1931; out of print since *c.* 1947.

Francis Grose's *Classical Dictionary of the Vulgar Tongue* (3rd edition, 1796), edited with biographical notice and a linguistic commentary, in a limited edition, 1931 – O.P. since *c.* 1948. A revised and unlimited general edition: Routledge & Kegan Paul; February 1963; 45s – U.S.: Barnes & Noble.

Name This Child: a dictionary of Christian or given names. 1936; 5th edition, 1959. (Hamish Hamilton; 5s – U.S.: British Book Centre; $1.50.)

A Dictionary of Slang and Unconventional English. 1937; 5th edition (7th printing, in all), revised and very much enlarged, in 2 vols., 1961. (Routledge; 105s – U.S.: Macmillan; $16.00.)

A New Testament Word-Book. 1940; O.P. since 1946.

A Dictionary of Clichés. 1940; 7th printing (4th edition, 4th impression), 1963. (Routledge; 12s 6d – U.S.: Macmillan; $2.75.)

A Dictionary of Abbreviations. 1942; 3rd edition, revised and enlarged, 1949. (Allen & Unwin; 8s 6d.)

A Dictionary of RAF Slang. 1945; O.P. since 1945.

Usage and Abusage: A Guide to Good English. 1947; 5th edition, revised and enlarged, 1957 – 4th impression, 1963. (Hamish Hamilton; 21s – U.S.: British Book Centre; $5.25.)

Shakespeare's Bawdy; A Literary and Psychological Essay and a Comprehensive Glossary. 1947, limited edition; 1956, general edition; 3rd edition, revised, 1958 – 2nd impression, 1962. (Routledge; 21s – U.S.: Dutton; $5.00.)

A Dictionary of Forces' Slang, with Wilfred Granville and Frank Roberts. 1948; O.P. since c. 1952.

Name into Word. 1949; 2nd edition, revised and enlarged, 1950; O.P. since c. 1954.

A Dictionary of the Underworld, British and American. 1950; 2nd edition, revised and enlarged, 1961. (Routledge; 70s – U.S.: Macmillan; $12.00.)

Chamber of Horrors: A Glossary of British and American Officialese, by 'Vigilans'; introduction by E. P. 1952.

(Andre Deutsch; 9s 6d – U.S.: Oxford University Press; $2.50.) A volume in 'The Language Library', edited by E. P.)

The Concise Usage and Abusage. 1954; 4th impression, 1963. (Hamish Hamilton; 10s 6d – U.S.: British Book Centre; $3.50.)

A First Book of Quotations, with Introduction. 1958; 2nd edition, revised, 1960. (Hamish Hamilton; 12s 6d – U.S.: British Book Centre; $3.75.)

Origins: An Etymological Dictionary of Modern English. October 1958; 3rd edition, revised and enlarged, December 1961—2nd impression, 1963 (Routledge; 90s – U.S.: Macmillan; $16.00.)

Shorter Slang Dictionary. 1961. (Routledge; 18s – U.S.: Macmillan; $4.00.)

Origins and *A Dictionary of Slang* became Mid-Century Book Society selections, the former in 1960, the latter in 1961; *Shakespeare's Bawdy,* a Dutton's Everyman Paperback in 1960; *Usage and Abusage,* a Penguin in 1963.